W9-AMZ-637

Global Communications
and Political Power

GLOBAL COMMUNICATIONS AND POLITICAL POWER

Donald Wilhelm

Transaction Publishers
New Brunswick (U.S.A.) and London (U.K.)

Library of Congress Catalog Number: 90-34812
ISBN: 0-88738-354-8
Printed in the United States of America

Library of Congress Cataloging-in-Publication Data

Wilhelm, Donald, 1915-
  Global communications and political power / Donald Wilhelm.
    p. cm/
  ISBN 0-88738-354-8
  1. Communication, International. 2. Communication policy--Soviet Union. 3. Soviet Union--Politics and government--1985- 4. Perestroika. I. Title
P96.I52S658 1990
302.2--dc20   90-34812

*This book is dedicated to all
those who so courageously spoke out
ahead of their time.*

Contents

Preface

The year 1977 saw the first publication, in Britain, of my book entitled *Creative Alternatives to Communism.*[1] In the book I argued that, although Marxist regimes then ruled a large share of the world, communism carried the seeds of its own destruction. It was already, I suggested, showing clear signs of its inherent instability and was giving advance signals of its inevitable decline in favour of more viable and humane systems. The work then set forth a range of non-communist options.

The book was subsequently published in the United States, in India, in Indonesia, and in a special edition for the Spanish-speaking world. But most important, brave people personally, and at no little risk to themselves (for the police states were still in the ascendency then), carried hundreds of copies of the work into the countries of Central and Eastern Europe. There, in its low-key and behind-the-scenes way, the book did its modest bit to provoke what was to become a tidal wave in support of freedom.

Recently, in what had been communist Central and Eastern Europe, we have seen an accelerating pace of change. Glasnost and perestroika have sufficiently taken root in the Soviet Union so that – at least in the

longer term and in spite of inevitable temporary set-
backs – they may prove to be irreversible. The hated
Berlin Wall has at last been breached, and the East
German regime has been largely transformed. Poland
has moved in the direction of becoming a multi-party
democracy, and Czechoslovakia has shown similar tendencies. In Hungary the ruling communist party has in
effect voted itself out of existence. Romania's totalitarian regime, which had held its people in an iron grip,
has been toppled by them. In 1990 the earlier-
omnipotent Soviet Communist Party, seeing the hand-
writing on the wall, surrendered its monopoly of power.
And so the signs multiply.

In all of this the communications revolution has
played, and will continue to play, a crucial role.
Through satellite and other communications we can
with our own eyes and in our own homes witness the
forward march of freedom; and in interactive fashion
those who strive for freedom receive fresh encouragement from the events thus portrayed. Yet the road to
the full achievement of parliamentary democracy,
human rights, economic and social well-being, and
international peace will continue to be a tortuous one,
and even the most sophisticated electronic media need
further intellectual complementation. Experience has
shown that works such as the present one are required
to help point the way.

In the writing of this book I am indebted to literally
hundreds of people – both those cited in the notes and
index and many others as well. Although it is impossible
properly to acknowledge all their courtesy and their
kindness, they will know of my indebtedness to them.
But exceptionally I must thank Dr. John Gunn for his
unstinting encouragement of the project; Professor

Irving Louis Horowitz and his staff at Transaction Publishers, Rutgers University; and Mike Graham-Cameron, my publishing consultant. I am eternally indebted to my wife Renée for inspiration, valuable thoughts, and perceptive assistance. Needless to say I alone am responsible for any errors of fact or interpretation.

DONALD WILHELM

Introduction

From the time he became Tsar in 1696, Peter the Great (1672–1725) made a determined effort to modernise Russia, and he brought in much Western expertise for this purpose. Much later, in the years leading up to World War I, Russia was industrialising very rapidly, again with the help of Western expertise. During most of the 1980s, Mikhail Gorbachev struggled – still with the aid of much expertise from the West – to modernise his ailing country with its laggard economy and under-developed political and social system. A brilliant man by any standard, he was in a certain allegorical sense a new Peter the Great.

More than seventy years after her creation as the world's first major Marxist state, the vast Soviet Union still cannot feed herself. Although ranked as a military superpower, she has a third-world economy. Increasingly the signs suggest that her empire – the only remaining one on earth – is coming apart at the seams.

That empire had grown rapidly both during and after World War II. During the war the Soviet Union had gobbled up much of independent Poland and all of the independent Baltic states of Estonia, Latvia, and Lithuania. At the ill-starred Yalta conference of 1945, the Soviet Union in effect received a free hand to dominate most of the remainder of Eastern Europe. It was of course Winston Churchill who, in the following year, sounded the first clear alarm when, in his definitive speech at Fulton, Missouri, he proclaimed that the Iron Curtain had descended across Europe.

But from the outset it became clear that the spirit of liberty had not been, and could not be, extinguished. The stirrings of freedom led Soviet forces to invade Hungary in 1956, the cultural obscenity of the Berlin Wall was created in 1961, and the Czechoslovakian tragedy was enacted in 1968. With the emergence in Poland in 1980 of Solidarity as communist Europe's first major independent trade union, a movement was established which refused to go away.

As conditions became increasingly unstable within the Soviet Union and its empire, the times in a real sense called forth the man – in the shape of Gorbachev. Having been born in 1931 in the southern Soviet Union village of Privolnoe, and having by the age of 15 started work as a harvester operator, Gorbachev had by 1967 received degrees both in law and in agriculture. His rise through the Communist hierarchy was swift, and by 1970 he had become a member of the USSR's Supreme Soviet, in 1983 he became General Secretary of the Communist Party of the Soviet Union, and in 1988 he was chosen as his country's President as well.

Meanwhile, in 1987, he had published his eloquent book entitled *Perestroika: New Thinking for Our Country and the World*.[1] The book offers a fascinating combination of astuteness together with intellectual provinciality. In the book Gorbachev provides, at one and the same time, a scathing denunciation of much that he finds wrong in his country plus a series of proposed remedies constructed within the confines of an ideological straightjacket. The work deserves the most careful and sympathetic examination together with a strong infusion of Western insights and perspectives.

Gorbachev himself may well be a passing phenomenon; the internal and external pressures on him are so enormous that he could disappear from the scene at any time. But, from the Western perspective, he symbolises an important milestone along the road to the emancipation of the vast Soviet empire. On the one hand he deserves the West's fullest support for the admittedly-still-inadequate reforms which he has implemented or attempted; and on the other hand his dynamic thrust should stimulate a powerful and supportive initiative from the West.

In a real sense we need to go over the heads of Gorbachev and his immediate successors in order to reinforce all available reform potentials. For this purpose we can employ a combination of cool rational analysis together with the galloping new global communications technology which can in the near future reach the great majority of people both in Eastern Europe and in the world at large. This book is largely concerned with that exciting global communications revolution; but first it is essential to understand what signals the Gorbachev phenomenon carries for the world.

1 The Perils of Perestroika

Mikhail Gorbachev, in his *Perestroika* book, forcefully sets forth what he sees as the symptoms of the Soviet Union's malaise. In the latter half of the 1970s, he points out, the country began to lose momentum. Stagnation "and other phenomena alien to socialism" began to appear. The economic growth rate declined. The economic gap between the Soviet Union and what he candidly refers to as "the world's advanced nations" began to widen still more. The consumer "found himself totally at the mercy of the producer and had to make do with what the latter chose to give him." Moreover, declining growth rates and economic stagnation "were bound to affect other aspects of the life of Soviet society." In consequence, continues Gorbachev, "A gradual erosion of the ideological and moral values of our people began."

The situation was indeed serious. "Problems snow-balled faster than they were resolved." The country verged on crisis.[1] Drastic remedies were called for. Gorbachev and his team therefore undertook a major restructuring both of the economy and – in a manner of speaking – the political system. The twin concepts of perestroika or restructuring and glasnost or openness were emphasised. As a result, according to Gorbachev,

1

Many things are unusual in our country now: election of managers at enterprises and offices; multiple candidates for elections to Soviets in some districts; joint ventures with foreign firms; self-financed factories and plants, state and collective farms; the lifting of restrictions on farms producing food products for enterprises and run by them; wider cooperative activities; encouragement of individual enterprise in small-scale production and trade; and closure of non-paying plants and factories operating at a loss; and of research institutes and higher educational establishments working inefficiently. A press that is more incisive, taking up 'taboos,' printing a rich variety of public points of view, and conducting an open polemic on all vital issues concerning our progress and perestroika. . . .[2]

Not surprisingly, as Gorbachev frankly confessed, "perestroika has proved more difficult than we at first imagined."[3] Often it seemed that whichever way he turned, the bureaucracy opposed him, and bureaucratic foot-dragging often appeared to be the rule rather than the exception. But the real trouble lay much deeper than that. Gorbachev himself took pains to emphasise that he was a communist following in the footsteps of Marx and Lenin, and there lay the root of his problem.

According to Gorbachev, "No matter what the opponents of Communism think, Communism originated and exists in the interests of man and his freedom, in order to defend his genuine rights, and justice on earth."[4] But according to Nobel Laureate Andrei Sakharov, well known both as a leading Soviet scientist and as a human rights activist, communism is an inadequate ideology ill-suited to the needs of his beloved home-land.[5] The respective merits of the two points of view have, one might say, been undergoing a scientific test.

Although Gorbachev pays tribute to Karl Marx (1818–1883) and to Marx's collaborator Friedrich Engels (1820–1895), his particular allegiance is to Marx's devout disciple Vladimir Ilyich Lenin (pseudonym of V. I. Ulyanov, 1870–1924). In his public utterances Gorbachev constantly eulogises Lenin, and in his *Perestroika* book he refers to Lenin *well over seventy times*, and always with admiration. Yet in terms of civilised humanity Lenin left much to be desired – both in his theory and in his practice.

Roland W. Clark, in his monumental and definitive biography of Lenin,[6] has with great care and objectivity uncovered that leader's thinking and his performance. After Russia's first and only democratic general election produced a minority of votes for Lenin's Bolshevik Party, Lenin successfully conspired to have the new National Assembly abolished by decree early in 1918. Later in that same year Lenin established the Extraordinary Commission for Combatting Counter-Revolution, Speculation and Sabotage – i.e., the Cheka secret police – which quickly developed into "the country's most feared organization." Lenin then used the Cheka to suppress all political parties apart from his own. He had successfully seized supreme power.[7]

Especially after an attack on Lenin's life in August 1918, there followed "a dramatic increase in the activities of the Cheka, which even during the preceding months had steadily been transforming isolated executions into a widespread and organized campaign soon rightly known as the Red Terror." As for Lenin's personal involvement, "There can be no doubt about

3

his knowledge and encouragement of the killings which took place by the thousand from the summer of 1918 onwards."[8]

As Clark rightly reminds us, terror "had a long ancestry in Russia, and from the mid-nineteenth century onwards both the tsarist authorities and many revolutionary groups used it in efforts to achieve their ends. . . ."[9] But Lenin and his dreaded Cheka extended and systematised the process more than was ever done by the nineteenth or twentieth century Tsars.

As Robert Conquest points out, Lenin had developed a theoretical justification for terror as early as 1905. Moreover, he "continually insisted on intensified terror against the judgement of many of his subordinates."[10] Lenin never forgot the theoretical – i.e., Marxist – rationale for terror. Thus in 1918, after alluding to misgivings even among hardened Bolsheviks at the excesses of the Cheka, Lenin stated:

> When we are reproached with cruelty, we wonder how people can forget the most elementary Marxism. . . . The most important thing for us to remember is that the Cheka is directly carrying out the dictatorship of the proletariat, and in this respect its services are invaluable.[11]

It is in this sense that Lenin's was a policy of cold *calculated* mass terror. With Lenin, Marx's "scientific socialism" provided a proper basis for what Clark has termed the "unqualified ruthlessness with which he was prepared to pursue his aims in the sacred cause of the Revolution." And he quotes a contemporary observer who referred to Lenin's "abstract social hatred and cold political cruelty."[12]

Many people forget that *it was Lenin, not Stalin, who*

inaugurated the Red Terror which flourished from early in the life of the new Soviet state. Moreover, *it was Lenin, not Stalin,* who first instituted the bizarre "show trials," leading to certain execution of the accused, which later became so characteristic of Stalin's rule.[13] The evidence for these statements is so compelling that nobody – including Gorbachev – can deny them.

Brilliant as a political strategist and tactician, Lenin became one of the chief architects of totalitarianism in its modern form. In fact he both antedated and surpassed Hitler as well as Mussolini in this respect. Lenin was indeed the great pioneer of modern totalitarianism.

In October 1988, an inaugural conference – sanctioned by Gorbachev and attended by some 600 people – met in Moscow to launch Memorial, a new organisation to honour the victims of Stalinism and for related purposes. Dr. Sakharov, one of the movement's steering committee, urged that Memorial should concern itself not only with Stalin's victims but also with those who suffered under Khrushchev and Brezhnev, Stalin's two main successors. And one writer who was present daringly referred to Lenin's own record as founder of the forerunner of the KGB and creator of the Soviet network of concentration camps known as the Gulag; and he bravely asked that Lenin's deeds should be investigated no less thoroughly than those of Stalin.[14]

Although Gorbachev had sent a message of support to the inaugural meeting of Memorial, clearly there was the danger that the movement could get out of hand. The Kremlin's leadership could not fail to be aware that for Memorial to be allowed such broad terms of reference might undermine the entire legitimacy of communist rule in the Soviet Union.

Clearly Gorbachev or his immediate successors faced

a serious dilemma which required a thorough rethink. The problem was highlighted by a painting, by a former Gulag prisoner, which was placed on display at Memorial's inaugural meeting. Comparing Stalin and Hitler, the painting depicts a large pile of human skulls surrounding Hitler and a much larger pile of human skulls surrounding Stalin.[15]

The evidence is clear that Lenin had misgivings about the choice of Stalin as his successor. In Lenin's so-called Testament, written shortly before his death, he says among other things that "Comrade Stalin, having become Secretary-General, has unlimited authority concentrated in his hands, and I am not sure whether he will always be capable of using that authority with sufficient caution. . . ."[16] And he even went on to suggest "that the comrades think about a way of removing Stalin from that post and appointing another man in his stead. . . ."[17] But that of course was not to be, and Stalin quickly consolidated his absolute power.

The reasons were obvious. Lenin, having constructed a totalitarian system and having ruthlessly presided over the growth of the Soviet police state, was almost bound to be followed by a leader who was equally ruthless if not more so. Lenin, as Clark suggests, "paved the way first for the enormities of the Cheka and then for the even greater enormities perpetrated by Stalin."[18]

In Conquest's summation,

It seems clear that the sacrifices of Lenin's and Stalin's rule – running into tens of millions of deaths, and other moral and physical suffering on a vast scale – could only be justified if they had produced a society incomparably superior to anything in the Russian past, anything in the

6

reformist West. Few would now argue that this has occurred.[19]

Gorbachev faces two fundamental problems, and the
same will apply to his immediate successors. In the first
place, he *has run out of heroes.* In this respect he has
boxed himself into a corner. In his *Perestroika* book he
makes clear that in his view none of the predecessor
Soviet leaders deserves either admiration or emulation
– with the sole exception of Lenin, upon whom he
heaps lavish praise. But any objective examination of
Lenin's record shows that he adroitly laid the ground-
work for the very sorts of excesses that were to follow
for decades.

So in terms of Soviet leaders worthy to be wor-
shipped, the cupboard is bare – from the time of
Lenin's Bolshevik Revolution at least until we come to
the incomplete verdict on Gorbachev himself. And the
reason the cupboard is bare is not far to seek. Gorbachev's second fundamental problem lies in the fact that
he stands for a flawed system. In the Soviet Union itself,
and virtually throughout the Soviet empire as well, the
system has proved defective.

Gorbachev, as a disciple of Marx and Lenin, could
not be more explicit as to where he stands ideologically. "Perestroika," he emphasises, "is closely con-
nected with socialism as a system." Moreover, he
insists, "I would like to point out once again that we
are conducting all our reforms in accordance with the
socialist choice. We are looking within socialism,
rather than outside it, for the answers to all the
questions that arise. We assess our successes and
errors alike by socialist standards. . . ."[20]

"More socialism," declares Gorbachev in a slightly

baffling broadside which seems to defy history, "means more democracy, openness and collectivism in everyday life, more culture and humanism in production, social and personal relations among people, more dignity and self-respect for the individual." In addition, "more socialism means more patriotism and aspiration to noble ideals. . . ."

"We want more socialism," says Gorbachev in a remarkable tour de force, "and, therefore, more democracy."[21] And to avoid any possible misunderstanding he makes the following sweeping assertion: ". . . We aim to strengthen socialism, not replace it with a different system. What is offered to us from the West . . . is unacceptable to us."[22]

It is illuminating to compare these views with those, already referred to, of Sakharov. Until the regime dismissed him in 1968 for his dissenting opinions, Sakharov was one of the Soviet Union's most influential and productive physicists; and indeed he deserves credit for having very largely fathered the powerful Soviet nuclear arsenal. But he had come to feel that the regime for which he worked was guided by a defective ideology. As he put it,

> One 'dogma of the faith' that has always figured in Soviet and pro-Soviet propaganda is the thesis of the uniqueness of the Soviet political and economic system, which (it is claimed) is the prototype for all other countries: the most just, humane, and progressive system, ensuring the highest standard of living, etc.

> The more obvious the complete failure to live up to most of the promises in that dogma, the more insistently it is maintained. . . .[23]

Moreover, he warns, "the dangers of totalitarianism associated with the socialist, so-called progressive path of development have been repeatedly and glaringly evident in recent times."[24]

In his brilliant book entitled *The Other Europe*, Jacques Rupnik remarks that "for conservative Russians, like Solzhenitsyn, the Communism that brought about the ruin of Russia was a Western import, a virus Lenin brought back from Zurich. . . ."[25] That virus was of course Marxism, which Lenin successfully introduced into Russia – even though Marx himself had thought that Russia was not yet sufficiently developed for it to be implanted there. Thus was born what we have already referred to as the world's first major Marxist state, and thus began a catalogue of political, economic and cultural disasters at the hands of Lenin and his successors.

If Marxism is indeed a flawed system, it is important to grasp the real nature of its fundamental shortcomings. At a pragmatic level one can say simply that – judging by the experience of the Soviet Union and the countries comprising its empire – Marxism simply does not work. But this diagnosis, while valid as far as it goes, remains superficial. The deeper question is this: *why* has Marxist ideology proved so defective? *Why*, in short, has Marxism been found wanting?

Many people, Marxists and non-Marxists alike, are not fully aware of what is actually the most vulnerable aspect of Marxist theory. Karl Marx himself hinted at that aspect in the following key passage in the first volume of his great work *Capital*:

Labour is, in the first place, a process in which both man and Nature participate, and in which man of his own accord starts, regulates, and controls the material reactions between himself and Nature. He opposes himself to Nature as one of her own forces, setting in motion arms and legs, heads and hands, the natural forces of his body, in order to appropriate Nature's production in a form adapted to his own wants. By thus acting on the external world and changing it, he at the same time changes his own nature. . . . He not only effects a change of form in the material on which he works, but he also realizes a purpose of his own . . . to which he must subordinate his will. . . .[26]

It shows Marx's intellectual power that he so clearly recognised the man/nature relationship and the importance of what elsewhere he identified as *the productive forces*. He viewed the productive forces as including (1) working people, (2) means of production as developed and employed by people, and (3) the raw materials and natural resources consumed in the productive process.[27]

In the second volume of *Capital*, Marx carried his fundamental analysis further as follows:

Whatever the social form of production, labourers and means of production always remain factors of it. But in a state of separation from each other either of these factors can be such only potentially. For production to go on at all they must unite. The specific manner in which this union is accomplished distinguishes the different economic epochs of the structure of society from one another.[28]

In *The Poverty of Philosophy*, Marx likewise wrote in similar vein:

Social relations are closely bound up with productive forces. In acquiring new productive forces men change

10

their mode of production, and in changing their mode of production . . . they change all their social relations. . . .[29]

Now it is of course well known that Marx laid great stress upon the notion of class and the class struggle; in *The Communist Manifesto*, for example, he and Engels gave pride of place to the declaration that "The history of all hitherto existing society . . . is the history of class struggles." This enabled them to develop the argument leading up to the famous call to action which formed the *Manifesto*'s climax: "WORKING MEN OF ALL COUNTRIES, UNITE!"[30]

In the view of Marx and Engels, the capitalist bourgeoisie "cannot exist without constantly revolutionizing the instruments of production, and . . . the whole relations of society." Crediting it with astonishing feats, they declared that the bourgeoisie,

> during its rule of scarce one hundred years, has created more massive and more colossal productive forces than have all preceding generations together. Subjection of Nature's forces to man, machinery, application of chemistry to industry and agriculture, steam-navigation, railways, electric telegraphs, clearing of whole continents for cultivation, canalization of rivers, whole populations conjured out of the ground – what earlier generation had even a presentiment that such productive forces slumbered in the lap of social labour?[31]

But the bourgeosie's very success, claimed Marx and Engels, would prove its undoing. "The productive forces at the disposal of society no longer tend to further the development of the conditions of bourgeois property; on the contrary, they have become too

11

powerful for those conditions. . . ." And again, "not only has the bourgeoisie forged the weapons that bring death to itself, it has also called into existence the men who are to wield those weapons – the modern class – the proletarians."[32]

Many commentators on Marxism have not fully appreciated the extent to which Marx's concept of the productive forces lies at the very heart of his system. The foregoing quotations help to make this point clear. Marx's analysis is widely assumed to be founded squarely on the famous concept of the class struggle, but actually that is *not a primary but a derivative concept*. Marx's own argument provides the evidence.

Although he attached such great importance to the productive forces, Marx never fully grasped the idea that those forces would themselves be deliberately and creatively reshaped by technology. Simplistically he envisaged a straight-line projection of the kind of machinery found in mid-nineteenth-century factories. The marvellous vitality and adaptability and diversification of science and technology seem largely to have escaped him.

Marx had, at his very elbow, dramatic proof of the liveliness and versatility of nineteenth-century Western technology, for it was while he was living and labouring in London that there occurred the Crystal Palace Exhibition – or Great Exhibition, as it was properly called – of 1851.[33] Here, arrayed in lavish profusion, were pieces of the new technology that was fast changing the character and fabric of Western society. One wonders if Marx ever left the British Museum, where he was steeped in his manuscripts, to visit the Great Exhibition. Certainly he failed to grasp the real character of the trend-setting technology which was transforming Western society and culture in varied and complex ways.

Marx's whole philosophy of history and of revolution hinges on the idea that the productive forces remorselessly became out of joint with the existing social organisation and that a violent social upheaval therefore ensues. It is essential, he contends, to manoeuvre the social organisation back into harmonious relationship with the productive forces, and violent revolution serves that purpose. It is this kind of philosophy which guided Lenin into and through his Bolshevik Revolution and which set in train the continuing excesses which were to follow.

The worship of such false idols as Marx and Lenin has had incalculable consequences for Central and Eastern Europe not to mention other parts of the world; and obviously that kind of worship undermines Gorbachev's whole position. By continually eulogising Lenin in particular, Gorbachev has placed himself in an intellectually untenable position – and one totally at variance with any enlightened view of human rights. Furthermore, the weakness in Gorbachev's intellectual stance will inevitably exacerbate the predicament of his immediate successors, for neither they nor many of their subjects will easily escape from the effects of prolonged "Newspeak" brain-washing in support of Lenin. But there will come a time when the truth will out, even throughout the length and breadth of the Soviet Union and its empire; and, as we shall see, the West can employ fresh means to facilitate this process.

In 1988, at the parade in Moscow's Red Square marking the 71st anniversary of the Bolshevik Revolution, even the customary portraits of Marx and Engels were missing; instead, a gigantic picture of Lenin

13

dominated the entire scene.[34] It is worth remembering that this was some three years after Gorbachev had achieved supreme power in the Soviet Union, and clearly such glorification of Lenin reflected Gorbachev's wishes. It is likewise worth remembering that, as Thom points out, it was Lenin, not Gorbachev, who pioneered the perestroika concept.[35]

It was in 1921 that Lenin, after his own monumental mismanagement of the Soviet economy had helped to bring it into renewed crisis, did a major tactical U-turn. Having remorselessly persecuted the kulaks, or more prosperous entrepreneurial farmers, and having had his men murder countless thousands of them together with their families, Lenin not surprisingly saw agricultural production plummeting and famine sweeping over the country. He then brought in his New Economic Policy or NEP, which Clark well calls "that great qualification of Bolshevik principles, which for a time revitalised the economy by diluting communal good with private profit."[36] In short, Lenin departed from his ideological principles through a major restructuring of the Soviet economy which temporarily restored profit incentives to the family farmer as well as to various other entrepreneurs.

As Winston Churchill wrote of Lenin's introduction of the NEP, "He repudiated what he had slaughtered so many for not believing. They were right it seemed after all. They were unlucky in that he did not find it out before."[37] And of course the perestroika was not to last, for under Stalin the kulaks were brutally dispossessed and collectivised in a wholesale return to "sound" Marxist principles.

Gorbachev, as Lenin's disciple, faces a dilemma somewhat comparable to that encountered by his predecessor

14

whom he so much admires. In his day, Lenin faced plenty of opposition from Party hardliners to his tactical moves in the direction of a market economy; and the same is of course true of Gorbachev today. Likewise a principal reason why Lenin brought in his NEP was to help woo the West into giving the Soviet Union more aid;[38] and the same is true of Gorbachev. Although a fully committed Marxist, Lenin felt obliged, at least for reasons of expediency, to make occasional departures from Marxist principles; and the same is true of Gorbachev.

In Geoffrey Hosking's assessment, the crisis which Gorbachev faces "is the crisis of Soviet totalitarianism. The system is undermining itself through its own inherent contradictions, putting at risk the great power status which it once achieved."[39] If and when Gorbachev is displaced as overall leader, his immediate successors will face essentially the same crisis.

If the crisis is as serious as Hosking suggests, then Gorbachev's opposition-ridden reform measures may become a case of too little and too late. It is true that Gorbachev's version of Soviet perestroika is considerably more diversified, far-reaching and sophisticated than was that of Lenin, but the same inner contradictions remain. Moreover, Gorbachev, much more than his hero Lenin, faces increasingly restless ethnic and nationality groups both within the Soviet Union and in its outer empire.

Perhaps one can best view the Soviet leadership question in terms of a sort of non-Marxist dialectic. Gorbachev and his immediate successors will press for reforms which will nominally fall within the Marxist framework. The leadership will for some time continue to advocate and uphold the flawed Marxist system. But

15

the dialectic of history will bring an ever-growing awareness of the total inadequacy of the ideology to which the leadership is committed. Eventually the flawed system will collapse both within the Soviet Union itself and throughout its captive empire.

When, in 1988, Britain's Prime Minister Margaret Thatcher visited the Polish city of Gdansk, thousands of workers shouted their greetings to her and their support of Solidarity. But with gusto they also yelled "Down with Communism!"[40] This rallying cry, increasingly heard in Central and Eastern Europe, helps to foretell the shape of the future.

2 Reinforcing Reform

As we have already found in Chapter 1, it was Lenin, not Gorbachev, who first introduced perestroika in the Soviet Union. But that is not all, for a much more enlightened form of perestroika was inaugurated in Czechoslovakia at the time of the "Prague Spring" in 1968, before Soviet and other Warsaw Pact forces engulfed the country and stifled all efforts at reform. Indeed, as Rupnik has aptly observed, "There is not a single new idea in Gorbachev's programme. All this has been said – and better – in the reform programme of the Prague Spring. . . ."[1] Being well aware that it was Russian tanks which defeated that perestroika programme, Gorbachev has never seen fit to acknowledge his indebtedness to it.[2]

After the rise of Solidarity in Poland in 1980–81, and the widespread euphoria surrounding it, the communist authorities of course staged a big crackdown against Solidarity. Such considerations as the foregoing have led Rupnik to make the following observations concerning the Central European region of the Soviet empire: "As all attempts at genuine internal change in the region have failed (1956 in Hungary, 1968 in Czechoslovakia, 1980–81 in Poland) the focus of people's hopes had tended to switch to external factors." With the dramatic rebirth of Solidarity in 1989 and the onrush of democracy throughout much of Central and Eastern Europe, this statement by Rupnik has on the face of it been overtaken by events. Yet Rupnik's "external factors" remain highly relevant; and perhaps foremost among such factors is the power of modern global communications.

Going further, Rupnik refers to "the defeat of the very idea of a fundamental reform of the system from within, and the ultimate proof of the impossibility of detotalizing totalitarianism. . . ."[3] This statement, too, must be modified in the light of events; and yet the struggle against totalitarianism and imperialism was bound to be a long and fluctuating one. In all parts of the empire the flame of resistance continued to burn, and this was well illustrated by the relatively tiny Baltic state of Estonia. In 1988 the Estonians demanded the right to veto laws enacted in Moscow, to form their own army, and even to secede from the Soviet Union. In 1989 the Supreme Soviet in Moscow actually approved a plan for the Baltic states to enjoy a degree of economic autonomy, but it remained to be seen how this would work out in practice.

It is quite clear that Gorbachev's version of perestroika has served to fan the flames of nationalism in diverse parts of the Soviet empire. As Hosking puts it, "The fact is – and Soviet leaders must face it squarely – the national question could break the Soviet Union."[4] Gorbachev having opened Pandora's box, one could wait to see what will happen; but that is indeed exactly what one should *not* do. The risks for the West, and for those who remain in a state of suppression within the empire, are simply too great.

Referring back to the time of the Teheran Conference in 1943, Rupnik correctly emphasises "the absence of any clear concept in Western strategic thinking."[5] That same characterisation has unfortunately continued to apply even to the present day. And with the Soviet empire in its deepest-ever ferment since the demise of Hitler, the need for an adequate Western strategical response becomes paramount.

Hosking suggests that the national question – or nationalism – has broken all the other empires of the twentieth century, and he asks why the Soviet empire should be an exception. In answer he believes that

> the strength of the armed forces and the security police gives it quite a good chance of being an exception. But all the same, if the Soviet leaders don't handle national aspirations with exemplary tact, then the only way they'll be able to hold the whole explosive mixture together is by combining super-Brezhnevian corruption with military and police coercion on a scale which would distract the Soviet Union from its strategic commitments. That would be expensive, demoralising and internationally enfeebling.[6]

As if the seething nationality question were not enough, the Soviet economy remained in dire straits. According to one estimate from within the Soviet Union itself, the country in 1988 ranked between 50th and 60th in the world in terms of goods and services consumed per head.[7] In that same year Leonid Abakkin, the head of the Institute of the Economy of the Soviet Academy of Sciences, stated that perestroika was "at a critical stage" and that it might take "decades" to implement it.[8]

Conceivably, as Tim Whewell has suggested, Gorbachev might become "the first ever Soviet leader whose rule will end neither in death nor disgrace."[9] And yet at the same time, in the context of the increasingly festering nationality question and in particular the demands of the Estonians for more autonomy and indeed for independence, Whewell intimates that it could "spell the beginning of the breakup of the Soviet empire."[10]

Should the West therefore now think the unthinkable? Should it plan decisive steps to bring about the early dismemberment of the Soviet empire? Such a plan, stated so baldly, would at first glance seem totally unrealistic. And yet the seeds have been planted and they are already growing. The West can quietly and skilfully nurture the seeds of liberation.

In 1988 – in a case of turning a poacher into a game-keeper if there ever was one – Gorbachev, in a shuffle of party functionaries, transferred Viktor Chebrikov from his post as head of the KGB to that of legal supremo entrusted with the task of creating a state based on the rule of law. Chebrikov meanwhile made the revealing statement that he believed that most Soviet citizens' demonstrations were caused by too much listening to Western radio broadcasts.[11] In similar vein it has been suggested that in spite of its longstanding opposition to Washington's Strategic Defense Initiative or "Star Wars" or SDI, the Kremlin is secretly more worried about Western direct broadcasting by satellite or DBS than it is about SDI.

We shall see more of these matters later in this book. But first it is important to gain a fuller understanding of Gorbachev's fundamental inconsistency with respect to the Soviet empire. In his *Perestroika* book, as we have already found, Gorbachev goes to great lengths to castigate Stalin and Stalinism; and exposing Stalin's crimes has indeed, under Gorbachev's stimulus, become very much a growth industry within the Soviet Union. But it was the now-despised Stalin who created the very Soviet empire which Gorbachev strives to keep intact. Gorbachev, in other words, faces the thankless task of trying to justify continued Soviet imperial domination over the selfsame countries which were confiscated in the first instance by the now-reviled Stalin and his henchmen.

The contradiction is so absurd as to be laughable but at the same time deadly serious. Gorbachev tries to eat his cake and have it too; on the one hand he seeks to rally his domestic constituency by constantly referring to the tyranny of Stalin, and on the other hand he attempts to justify continued Soviet control over the empire carved out by that same tyrant. People all over Eastern Europe, and throughout the world at large, will more and more become aware of this fundamental and intellectually untenable inconsistency.

It is important to look back on how Stalin gained his empire, for this can furnish further evidence on why it should be dismembered and by what means. As Michael Dockrill points out,[12] even as early as at the 1943 Teheran conference, Roosevelt and Churchill managed to leave Stalin with the impression that he had been given a free hand in Eastern Europe in return for various other concessions. Moreover, both Roosevelt and Churchill came away from the conference believing that they could trust Stalin; and indeed Roosevelt, in a glowing report to the U.S. Congress, predicted that "we are going to get along well with him and the Russian people – very well indeed."[13]

Later came the full-dress Yalta conference of 1945 in

the Crimea, at which a combined British and American delegation of some 700 people were present. Understandably the conference has been called another Munich. Roosevelt was now a dying man, his personality seemed to have changed, and he and Churchill found themselves unable to collaborate fully. Churchill was full of foreboding and soon afterwards he wrote that "I could only feel the vast manifestation of Soviet and Russian imperialism rolling forward over helpless lands."

The summit meeting produced a communiqué which included a Declaration on Liberated Europe in which the following key passage was incorporated:

> The establishment of order in Europe and the rebuilding of national economic life must be achieved by processes which will enable the liberated peoples to destroy the last vestiges of Nazism and Fascism and to create democratic institutions of their own choice. This is a principle of the Atlantic Charter — the right of all peoples to choose the form of government under which they will live.[15]

As Pratt points out, "The promise of free elections open to all democratic elements in . . . liberated Europe sounded fair and generous. No one as yet realized that the Russians would equate democracy with acceptance of Communism and would enforce this view ruthlessly wherever the fortunes of war had given them the power."[16]

In Rupnik's view, "Yalta was not a conspiracy to divide Europe, but it contributed to the legitimization of Soviet control in East-Central Europe in return for promises that were never kept, nor were meant to be." And he refers to "the inherent contradictions of policies based on mistaken assumptions about Stalin and the Soviet system."[17] In particular he notes the following gross oversight on the part of the Allies:

> . . . It was clear – to anybody who had cared to observe Soviet behaviour in the occupied countries in 1940 – that Stalin's 'security' concerns went beyond a traditional territorial concept of spheres of influence towards the goal of political control. For security reasons you create a buffer zone stretching a thousand kilometres west of your borders, and since the conquest is likely to breed resentment and thus 'insecurity' you put in charge only 'trustworthy' governments which, by definition, are those run by Communists. In this way military presence led to political and ideological absorption. . . .[18]

It quickly became apparent, as Pratt remarks, that "the Soviets had no intention of keeping their Yalta promises when they could gain by breaking them."[19] Referring to the Yalta Declaration on liberated Europe, George F. Kennan goes so far as to say that it "was, of course, a futile gesture, and one which no doubt would have been better avoided. Churchill and Roosevelt had no excuse for not knowing, by this time, that all this vague and general political terminology had one meaning to them and an entirely different one to Stalin. . . ."[20] "In retrospect," as J. Robert Wegs suggests, "the Yalta Declaration must be seen as a rather naive document."[21]

As Rupnik well emphasises, the events leading up to Yalta "reflected a failure of Allied strategic thinking."[22] Further such failures occurred after Yalta and have continued right up to the present day. Simplistic Western conceptions of Gorbachev and Gorbachevism provide an excellent case in point.

Western euphoria surrounding the Gorbachev phenomenon is well known. Yet at the end of 1988 *The Economist*, the highly-respected London-based journal, felt constrained to forecast as follows:

By the mid-1990s both Gorbachev and Gorbachevism may have been discarded. After nearly four years in power Mr. Gorbachev has not yet found a way of either getting his farms to grow more food or making his factories jump to the discipline of real competition. To the increasing discontent of Soviet consumers is now added a series of nationalist upheavals within the Soviet Union itself, all the way from Estonia to Armenia, and growing doubts about the durability of Russia's control over Eastern Europe. Mr. Gorbachev's chances of fighting his way through all these difficulties are not good.

If, suggested the journal, Gorbachev should fail, then his successor might very likely be a hardliner, "and Europe's guard will have to be up again." If, on the other hand, Gorbachev should succeed,

his definition of success offers little comfort to Europe. A Gorbachev success spells a richer Russia, which could spend more on its army without starving its consumers. It would still be a one-party, largely non-capitalist Russia, carrying the banner for a political philosophy hostile to the West's. The shadow Russia casts on people living west of the Elbe will not shrink unless sheer necessity pushes Mr. Gorbachev into dissolving Leninism and dismantling Russia's empire. Short of that, Europe will have to go on worrying about Russia.[23]

In addition to his practical problems, Gorbachev faces an acute intellectual dilemma. As we have already seen, he eulogises Lenin even though Lenin became a true tyrant and the godfather of Stalin's even more massive subsequent abuses. Gorbachev condemns Stalin even though Stalin constructed the empire which Gorbachev seeks to preserve.

As Thomas Sherlock points out, the reevaluation of the Soviet past can prove a dangerous thing. He explains that in 1986, "as Gorbachev came to perceive the need for broad social and political reform in the Soviet Union, he apparently began to perceive the utility of a broad re-examination of Soviet history." It appears that Gorbachev had three reasons for this: to enhance the collective ability to assess the health and coherence of the Soviet system; to undermine bureaucratic and popular resistance to reform; and to win the support of the intelligentsia for the reform programme.[24]

Soviet historians have been quick to take advantage of Gorbachev's encouragement, but this carries serious risks for the regime if not for the individual historians as well. For example, the eminent Soviet historian Roy Medvedev has actually published an extended critique of Lenin's concept of the dictatorship of the proletariat. As Sherlock suggests, when the Soviet historical endeavour "begins to criticize Lenin and Marxism-Leninism, it weakens the central ideological support of the reform program, which is described as 'a return to Leninism.'"[25] In terms of the regime's intellectual solvency, the whole process becomes hazardous in the extreme. And yet the more Gorbachev emphasises his concept of glasnost, the more difficult will it be to halt such dangerous and even regime-threatening intellectual activities.

Meanwhile the West cannot afford to shirk its own

25

need for reevaluation of its response to the evolving Soviet challenge. We have already noted Rupnik's trenchant comment that the West has lacked a clear strategy, and it is worth reviewing the West's post-Yalta response pattern with the idea of improving upon it in the light of emerging needs.

It was of course Yalta, and the events leading up to Yalta, which largely ushered in the Cold War. A convenient definition of the Cold War is that suggested by John W. Spanier: "The conflict between the Communist nations led by the Soviet Union and the Western nations led by the United States, fought by all means — ideological, economic, political, and limited military action — short of total war."[26] Because of the advent of nuclear weapons, it no longer seemed feasible to engage in total war, and both sides therefore resorted to the foregoing "cold" means of conflict.

Laqueur has admirably summarised as follows the intellectual confusion which arose in Western minds after Stalin's demise in 1953:

Stalin's death and the gradual disappearance of the worst features of his regime gave rise to high hopes in the West: the end of the cold war was believed to be at hand, and a new era of détente and peaceful coexistence seemed to have dawned over a continent torn by bitter strife. Such optimism was only natural; the international climate was bound to improve. . . . But the optimism prevailing at the time in the western capitals was not altogether warranted; to a certain extent it was based on a misjudgement of the motives of Soviet policy, on the mistaken belief that 'cold war' and 'peaceful coexistence' were mutually exclusive policies, whereas in fact they were only different aspects of Soviet foreign policy. . . .[27]

Nikita S. Khrushchev's dramatic rise to power in the 1950s provided a foretaste of Gorbachev's swift rise to supreme power in the 1980s. In 1956 Khrushchev denounced Stalin in a way that almost provided the script for Gorbachev's own later condemnation of Stalin. Khrushchev likewise anticipated Gorbachev when he proclaimed and progressively implemented a programme of de-Stalinisation including a relaxation of the stifling cultural climate, with even the great dissident Solzhenitsyn being allowed to publish in the Soviet Union. Khrushchev further provided a future game-plan for Gorbachev when he repeatedly made sweeping demands for world disarmament.

It is perhaps symbolically significant that in the same year, 1956, in which Khrushchev denounced Stalin, he presided over the invasion of Hungary. It was likewise of course under Khrushchev's ascendency that the Berlin Wall was constructed in 1961 and the Cuban missile crisis occurred in 1962. Meanwhile he had presided over a series of economic reverses at home. In 1964 Khrushchev abruptly fell from power; and two days after his dismissal *Pravda* denounced his "hare-brained scheming, immature conclusions, hasty decisions, and actions divorced from reality." As Wegs points out, failures in both domestic and foreign policy led to Khrushchev's fall, and a decisive factor may have been his having alienated the entrenched bureaucracy through political reforms akin to those which Gorbachev has been attempting.[28]

Of special interest for our present purposes is Khrushchev's concept of peaceful coexistence, which he unveiled in 1954 along with his denunciation of Stalin. Paradoxically, as Marshall D. Shulman points out, Khrushchev had borrowed the concept from Stalin himself.[29] Stalin had decided to initiate the peaceful coexistence policy for various compelling reasons including the West's initial nuclear supremacy, the growing moral authority of the United Nations, the Truman Doctrine, the Marshall Plan, the creation of NATO, the success of the Berlin airlift, and the military response of the United Nations in Korea. Stalin hoped that he had found in the concept a new kind of weapon.

Khrushchev, while castigating the author of the concept, nevertheless eagerly embraced it as if it were his own. But at the same time he condemned those who tried to extend coexistence into the ideological sphere. At the Twentieth Congress of the Communist Party of the Soviet Union, in 1956, Khrushchev declared:

> It does not follow at all from the fact that we stand for peaceful coexistence and economic competition with capitalism that the struggle against bourgeois ideology, against bourgeois survivals, can be relaxed. Our task is tirelessly to expose bourgeois ideology, reveal how inimical it is to the people, and show up its reactionary nature.[30]

Subsequently, Khrushchev stated even more publicly and bluntly what he meant and didn't mean by peaceful coexistence. Thus, on a state visit to Sweden in 1964, he declared that ideological coexistence would not become possible until Communism was everywhere triumphant. Later in that same year, he gave a still tougher meaning to peaceful coexistence. In the nuclear age, he asserted, the Soviet Union was opposed to wholesale war but not to wars of national liberation in which people sought to throw off their oppressors. And he made it clear that such "oppressors" included any sort of non-communist regime.

Gorbachev, evidently believing that the peaceful coexistence concept and terminology have lost some of their original lustre, has, in his persuasive *Perestroika*, restated them in a more mellow form as follows:

Economic, political and ideological competition between capitalist and socialist countries is inevitable. However, it can and must be kept within a framework of peaceful competition which necessarily envisages cooperation. It is up to history to judge the merits of each particular system. It will sort out everything. Let every nation decide which system and which ideology is better. Let this be decided by peaceful competition, let each system prove its ability to meet man's needs and interests. The states and peoples of the earth are very different, and it is actually good that they are so. This is an incentive for competition. This understanding, of a dialectical unity of opposites, fits into the concept of peaceful coexistence.[31]

When Stalin first initiated his concept of peaceful coexistence, he did it, as we have seen, for several compelling reasons. Gorbachev is likewise aware of certain contemporary compelling reasons, and chief among these is of course the current availability of weapons capable of universal destruction. This, he explains, has actually led the Communist Party of the Soviet Union to make an adjustment in its definition of peaceful coexistence of states with different social systems: party faithfuls can now delete the notion that this represents a specific form of class struggle.[32] Since Marx must be maintained, the class struggle can manifest itself in other ways.

Stalin of course followed in Lenin's footsteps and further expanded the scope of Lenin's brutal dictatorship;

and Gorbachev has, as we have seen, drawn his chief inspiration from Lenin. Ironically, in Khrushchev's day – and more recently in Gorbachev's time as well – the common Western tendency has been to relapse into a bland ideology-free view of so-called peaceful coexistence: both sides said they wanted to do it peacefully, so why worry about ideology?

At the beginning of the 1960s, when Khrushchev was flourishing and before he was sacked and became officially a non-person, Daniel Bell, an American author, published his famous book entitled *The End of Ideology*.[33] To a remarkable degree the book managed to forecast and capture the spirit of what has since been called the Simplistic Sixties; even the book's very title struck an instant responsive chord with many people in the West who had never read it or even seen it. For it seemed to suggest an end to old dogmas and outworn creeds and a refreshing new reliance upon pragmatic experience.

Through a series of painful lessons, the West has learned the futility of pragmatically reacting to events without the help of any general strategy. This has found no better illustration than in the case of America's failure in Vietnam, when a so-called superpower suffered the worst politico/military defeat in her history. General Vo Nguyen Giap, the chief architect (along with Ho Chi Minh as President of North Vietnam) of the final communist victory over America and her allies in Indo-China, was thoroughly explicit about his highly-developed overall strategy. In his *People's War, People's Army*,[34] Giap gave highest priority to the concept of *the primacy of the political*. Unlike his adversaries, he concentrated on matters far removed from heavy bombers, fighter planes, and helicopter gunships; indeed for most of his victorious campaign, Giap had very little of such sophisticated weaponry. Instead, he had reached a high level of sophistication in endowing men with a steadfast and seemingly unstoppable will to win. His victory was completely decisive and led to an enduring sense of American humiliation.

This example is offered merely as an illustration of the need for a convincing Western strategy or stable of strategies. How, for example, should the West deal with the Gorbachev phenomenon? A careful comparison of the Khrushchev and Gorbachev scenarios might well note that both men were shrewd and crafty operators; both pilloried Stalin; both attempted major cultural thaws; both sought comprehensive internal economic reforms; both launched bold foreign initiatives; and both collided with an entrenched Party hierarchy which plotted their removal from power. The analysis might well conclude that Gorbachev would almost automatically share Khrushchev's fate: to fall from grace and to be relegated to the role of a non-person.

Such an analysis might be pursued at great length and still come out with the same general conclusion. But one thing the analysis would certainly have to consider is this: the response of the West. Although Khrushchev's contacts with the West were often stormy, there were periods of considerable cordiality. For example, a summit meeting in Geneva between Khrushchev and several Western leaders in 1955 went so well that commentators for some time thereafter referred to "the spirit of Geneva." A meeting which Khrushchev had with President Eisenhower at Camp David in 1959 became so friendly that references were made to "the spirit of Camp David." One of the low points in East-West relations was reached in 1960, shortly before a summit meeting was due to take place in Paris. A high-flying U-2 American reconnaissance plane was shot down over the Soviet Union, and in his fury Khrushchev cancelled both the summit meeting and a planned visit by Eisenhower to Moscow.[35] Ironically such high-level reconnaissance planes were already becoming virtually obsolete because of the advent of satellite surveillance.

Now a key finding in such an analysis would be that at no point did the West make any systematic effort to help Khrushchev to achieve overdue and much-needed reforms at home. It is true that his meetings with Western leaders – including various concessions he won from them – may well have enhanced his stature within the Soviet Union. It is likewise true that various cultural and technical and trade arrangements which the West made with Khrushchev may have helped to improve his standing at home. It is furthermore true that Khrushchev's brash and irascible nature made him perhaps a dubious coexistence partner at the best of times. But the fact remains that the West did very little to bolster his efforts to reform the Soviet system.

With Gorbachev the situation is somewhat different. He (not to mention his wife Raisa) is more cosmopolitan than was Khrushchev, and in his personality he gives the impression of being somewhat steadier and more reliable than was Khrushchev. Moreover, major technological changes have occurred since Khrushchev's day, and fresh avenues have been opened up which will allow the West to play a much greater role in influencing the shape of the Soviet system. Indeed, as we shall see, it has now become possible for the West to go over the heads of Soviet leaders – whether Gorbachev or his successors – to appeal directly to the mass of the people both within the Soviet Union and throughout its empire.

That empire, as created by Stalin, remains an obscenity, and there is no possible justification for its continuation. In the case of the British and French empires, for example, the mother country was in most respects more advanced than its colonies; and in spite of shortcomings and abuses Britain and France did much to develop their colonies. In the case of the Soviet Empire, however, the situation is reversed, for most of the captive countries are in major respects more advanced than the Soviet Union itself. The Soviet Union indeed remains an underdeveloped country both politically and economically, and it is a complete nonsense for it to claim imperial domination over the countries which Stalin seized by force or dictatorial means. Moreover, even within the Soviet Union itself there is no possible justification for continued Kremlin control over regions such as the Baltic states which were won by Stalin through a triumph of treachery. These points can be judiciously broached.

In a very real sense, as we shall find, the West can go over Gorbachev's head to help ensure his own survival as leader. And if, as is not at all impossible, he should meet a fate not unlike that of Khrushchev, then the West can continue to exert a powerful constructive impact no matter who succeeds him.

3 The Satellite Explosion

In 1957 the Russians astonished the West by launching Sputnik 1, the world's first satellite and the first man-made object ever to be launched into outer space. In spite of economic adversities they have never looked back, and in the 1980s their expenditures on space have greatly exceeded those in the public sector of the United States. The Soviet Union has achieved the world's highest rate of successful space launches and she must indeed be ranked as *the world's leading space power*.[1] But the West has not been idle in the space field, and meanwhile the political and cultural implications of space have become ever more discernible.

It is well known that many animals have highly-developed means of communication. In man's own evolution from the Stone Age to the Space Age, his means of communication have developed apace. Essential to this process was of course the early acquisition of rudimentary forms of language, including sign language and so-called body language. Ancient cave-dwellers were among those who developed pictorial means of communication, and formalised alphabets and writing in due course evolved. But the problem of proper writing surfaces soon reared its head. Stone, clay, wood, lead, copper and brass were among the materials employed, but these were heavy and bulky. Large leaves such as those of the palm might be utilised, but these were perishable. Moreover, as Harry E. Neal points out, such materials as the foregoing made it virtually impossible for a scribe to make corrections or changes in his text. The early Romans, he suggests,

> were probably the first to remedy this . . . difficulty by coating flat pieces of wood with wax and then cutting their inscriptions into the wax. If changes were necessary it was a simple matter to 'erase' a letter or word or sentence by smoothing over the wax . . . and then [to] write the revision on the smoothed portion. A message could be cut into the wax and sent to a person in another town, who could read it, smooth it over, and write his reply on the same waxed board. . . .[2]

Here we have something which, in the sense of being a two-way message system, is rather in the spirit of the present-day fax machine. But it was the Egyptians who scored a great breakthrough with their development of papyrus writing paper. Papyrus is a tall-growing water plant which flourished in the shallow waters of the Nile and from which the Egyptians cut long narrow strips which they interwove, soaked, pounded, dried in the sun, and smoothed with a piece of shell or stone. The result was a superb and durable writing surface of which many examples have survived for thousands of years. In spite of the use of different raw materials, the paper-making technology evolved by the ancient Egyptians has much in common with that of the modern multinational paper industry.

Men have long realised the importance of delivering

written or other messages in minimum time. A shouted command or other oral message could be delivered promptly over a short distance, but long-range messaging called for more ingenuity. For example, in the days of the Persian empire (which at its height, about 500 B.C., covered most of the present-day Middle East), royal couriers, using closely spaced relay stations with fresh horses ready at each, could span the empire within fifteen days; and chains of regularly spaced semaphore towers stretching across the countryside permitted even more rapid communication. Much later, the inventor Claude Chappe (1763–1805) developed an improved semaphore system which was first used at the time of the French Revolution; with the aid of towers built at suitable intervals he was able to send messages 450 miles from Paris to the fleet in Toulon in 20 minutes.[3]

The advent of the printing press of course greatly enhanced the scope of communication. It appears that the Chinese, as early as 868 A.D., were the first to use movable type, in the shape of carved wooden blocks. It was not until about 1440 that movable type was apparently independently developed in Germany either by Johann Gutenberg or one of his associates, and the printing of the first of the famous Gutenberg Bibles seems to have been completed in about 1456. Some scholars claim that printing with movable type may have been developed in Holland at an earlier time, but in any event it spread very rapidly. In the Western world virtually all books were printed in Latin until about 1476, when in an historic development printing in English was introduced by William Caxton of Kent.

"The art of printing," as Neal remarks, "helped to bring the 'Dark Ages' of ignorance and superstition in

36

Europe to an end. New ideas spread far and wide by means of the printed word."[4] Moreover, it was printing, together with a whole range of additional communication technologies that were to come, which propelled the English language onto the world stage and increasingly gave it the role of the one universal language.

The interest in speeding up communication was to continue unabated, and this among other things led to incipient forms of postal services. As early as about 3800 B.C., the then king of Babylon had entrusted "letters," in the shape of inscribed clay tablets, to relays of runners who carried them across the country. In the fifth century B.C., Herodotus, the Greek historian, wrote as follows about men on horseback who carried messages inscribed on bronze tablets: "Neither snow, nor rain, nor heat, nor gloom of night stays these couriers from the swift completion of their appointed rounds."[5] Much later, the U.S. postal service embraced this as its motto.

The Emperor Diocletian inaugurated a limited public postal service in Rome around 300 A.D.; but after Rome's fall the concept lapsed and it was not until the sixteenth century that proper public postal services were established in France, Germany, and Britain. In 1784 England's first mail-coach service was started; the coach ran between London and Bristol and covered the nearly 120 miles in sixteen hours. But faster means of movement were desired, and the need soon called forth new technology.

In 1825 a steam locomotive, designed and built by George Stephenson, hauled both passengers and mail at the astonishing speed of twelve miles per hour. This was the beginning of the vast railway industry with tracks spanning many parts of the globe and with the carrying of mail as one of its key roles. In 1918 the world's first regular air-mail service was established between Washington, D.C. and New York City.[6] But electrical and electronic means had already been recognised as offering far more scope for high-speed messaging.

Communication took a great leap forward with the invention of the electric telegraph, especially the version perfected by Samuel F. B. Morse, an American portrait artist turned technologist. In 1844 Morse and his team completed the construction of a telegraph line between Washington and Baltimore, and over it was sent, in Morse code, the famous message, "What hath God wrought?" This was the first message sent over the first public telegraph line in the world, and the use of the telegraph soon spread by leaps and bounds. Submarine telegraphy before long began in earnest, with a cable being laid under the English Channel in 1851 and a transatlantic cable being completed in 1866.[7] These cables carried telegraphic messages by wire and soon it would become possible to send likenesses of the human voice by wire as well.

The principal inventor of the telephone was of course Alexander Graham Bell, a Scotsman who had migrated to Boston, Massachusetts. In 1876 Bell and his assistant Thomas A. Watson obtained a U.S. patent for the instrument, which later in that same year was exhibited at the Philadelphia Centennial Exhibition. In 1878, while on a honeymoon trip to England, Bell was invited to demonstrate his invention to Queen Victoria, who was so taken with it that she had a private line installed from the Isle of Wight to London. A few months later, the world's first general telephone service began operations in London.[8]

Although the telephone soon became a phenomenal success, men had already been groping for some way to achieve the rapid transmission of messages over long distances without wires. In 1894 Guglialmo Marconi, the Italian inventor, who was then only twenty years old, began experiments aimed at sending messages without wires. In the following year he succeeded in sending crude radio signals over two miles. He then took his findings to London and to Britain's Post Office Telegraph Department. Sir William Preece, the director of that department, displayed remarkably non-bureaucratic behaviour when in 1897 he arranged for Marconi to give a demonstration of his invention before a group of government officials. Before a distinguished audience Marconi showed that he could send clear electrical signals over a distance of several hundred yards without wires.

At the request of the Italian navy, Marconi then installed his radio equipment in some of their warships and showed that he could send messages between ships twelve miles apart. Then came the great challenge, for he was determined to try to send radio messages across the Atlantic from Cornwall to Newfoundland. This he managed to do in 1901, using a receiving aerial suspended some 400 feet in the air from a kite.[9] The age of long-distance radio communication could be fairly said to have begun.

Marconi of course sent his early radio messages by Morse code, but soon it became possible to employ the human voice as well. Numerous scientists and inventors had a hand in the development of radio broadcasting, and notable among these was Lee DeForest, who perfected and patented the radio tube or valve which permitted great amplification of weak radio signals.

39

Although there is considerable dispute as to when the human voice was first broadcast by radio, it is known that a Christmas Eve broadcast of talk and music took place in Massachusetts in 1906; that British Navy technicians transmitted "God Save the King" from one ship to another in 1907; and that DeForest broadcast a performance from the Metropolitan Opera House in New York in 1910. The first commercially licensed radio was KDKA in Pittsburgh, which commenced operations in 1920, and in Britain the first such station went on stream in 1922.[10]

Contributing to the dramatic worldwide spread of radio broadcasting has of course been the transistor as invented by a team at the Bell Telephone Laboratories in 1948. It has permitted far more compact and durable radio broadcasting and receiving equipment, and cheap transistor radios are now found on every part of the planet regardless of the prevailing political or social system. The transistor likewise plays a key role in the field of television including broadcasting by satellite.

A number of pioneers, whose work dates back even to the nineteenth century, helped pave the way to television. In 1915 Marconi forecast that there would one day be a "visible telephone". But the greatest of the television pioneers was undoubtedly a Scottish parson's son named John Logie Baird. In 1925, in London, he for the first time actually transmitted the likeness of a human face from one room to an adjoining room. Three years later, from Baird's studio, the British Broadcasting Corporation made the world's first public television broadcast. The BBC continued with experimental broadcasts and in 1936 it launched the first regular public television service in the world. This landmark event was to have enormous political and cultural repercussions of which we are still only beginning to be properly aware.

These early broadcasts were of course in black and white, and inventors had meanwhile been trying to develop colour television. After initial encouraging experiments by Baird in Britain, the Bell Telephone Laboratories in 1929 sent colour television pictures over a wire in New York. In 1940 two other American companies made test colour television broadcasts,[11] and broadcasting in colour gradually spread throughout the world.

Multinational television linkages were meanwhile taking shape. For example, by 1959 twelve countries in Western Europe had joined in the Eurovision network.[12] But it was the advent of communications satellites which enabled television broadcasting to become an integrated global enterprise. The 1957 launching of the world's first satellite was of course preceded by many centuries of thought and experimentation. Rockets were first used for military purposes by the Chinese in about 1100 A.D. and were encountered by British forces in India in the eighteenth century. In the nineteenth century rockets found extensive use by various European armies; and in the first half of the twentieth century an especially devastating form of rocket was the V2 with its one-ton warhead as used by the Germans to attack the London area in the Second World War.

Concurrently Arthur C. Clarke, a brilliant British radar expert, was clearly delineating the concept of sending rocket-launched communications satellites into outer space in order to extend the reach of television broadcasting. He pointed out that three such satellites, correctly spaced in "stationary" orbit in relation to the earth's rotation, could provide global television coverage. Because the transistor had not yet been invented, Clarke visualised the need for very large satellites manned by crews to replace defective tubes or valves.[13] But in fact, as we have seen, the transistor was to be unveiled very soon afterwards and unmanned communications satellites became entirely feasible.

The proliferation of man-made satellites in outer space has been nothing less than phenomenal. By the end of 1986, some 3500 satellites were already in orbit. Only about 40 of these were Western European ones; and of the remainder, the overwhelming majority belonged either to the Soviet Union or the United States, with the Soviet Union having the lion's share. As a definitive report by an international task force has pointed out, "The total number of satellites launched annually by the Soviet Union is approximately *three times greater than that of all other countries combined.*"[14] Many of the Soviet satellites are of course for military purposes, but many are not; and as we shall see, a subtle interaction exists between so-called defence satellites and so-called civilian ones.

According to Mark Long, "satellites have forever altered the common perception of the world. . . ." Our planet, he adds, "is encircled by a ring of man-made satellites that generate an invisible electromagnetic web. This web bonds our world together with a continuous exchange of video, audio, and data information."[15] With regard to the video side alone, it is worth comparing these comments with a statement made as far back as 1931, before communications satellites were even on the drawing boards. In that year the then U.S. Federal Radio Commissioner, H. A. Lafount, said, "I believe that television is destined to become the greatest force in the world. I think it will have more influence over the lives of individuals than any other force."[16] Although Lafount wisely refrained from predicting when this forecast might come true, certainly the advent of the communications satellite has rendered it all the more plausible.

A communications satellite of course normally receives video or other signals from a ground-level transmitter or uplink. The satellite then usually relays the signals back to appropriate ground-level receivers. In recent years, as Long points out, "the costs of commercial and home satellite receiving systems have fallen dramatically while quality has increased by leaps and bounds."[17] Meanwhile, as we have seen, the number of orbiting satellites has grown enormously. Among the multitude of satellites, those intended primarily for civil purposes fall into four main categories as follows: (A) the Intelsat global satellite system; (B) the Soviet satellite system; (C) the Inmarsat maritime satellite system; and (D) regional satellite systems including Eutelsat, Arabsat, and Palapa.

The advent of the Intelsat global satellite communications system represented, in its scale and scope, something entirely new under the sun. As Long well describes it,

On August 20, 1964, eleven countries signed a charter creating the International Telecommunications Satellite Organization (Intelsat), the first worldwide satellite communications network. Intelsat began offering transatlantic services in 1965 after the successful deployment of Intelsat I (Early Bird), the world's first commercial geostationary satellite. Today, fourth- and fifth-generation Intelsat birds provide international and domestic communications services on behalf of 112 member nations.[18]

The Intelsat network includes more than 700 earth stations at more than 500 different sites in 159 countries. Intelsat's space fleet includes fifteen satellites in geosynchronous equatorial orbits centred over the Atlantic, Pacific and Indian oceans for transoceanic telecommunications traffic. Intelsat's global traffic load *doubles about every five years,* and this calls for satellites with ever greater capacity. Many of these satellites are equipped with both high-powered spot beams and wide-ranging global beams.[19] The ongoing voyages of the Intelsat space fleet, and its ever-growing communications "payloads" – including its globe-girdling television linkages – portend the most profound cultural consequences.

At the same time one can scarcely dismiss the satellite telecommunications outreach of the Soviet Union as the world's leading space power. In addition to its formidable military presence in space, the Soviet Union has entered into civil space activities in a very big way. The Soviet answer to Intelsat has been Intersputnik, which it and collaborating countries formed in 1971 as an international satellite cooperative. Intersputnik includes fourteen member countries as follows: Afghanistan, Bulgaria, Cuba, Czechoslovakia, the German Democratic Republic, Hungary, the Korean People's Democratic Republic, Laos, Mongolia, Poland, Romania, the Soviet Union, the Socialist Republic of Vietnam, and the People's Republic of Yemen. In addition, non-members such as Algeria, Iraq, Libya, Nicaragua and Syria sometimes use the Intersputnik network for communication with member countries. As Long points out,

The Russian satellite system conceivably can beam radio, TV programs, voice, and data traffic to almost any location on earth. Of the world's numerous domestic, regional, and international satellite systems, only Intelsat can supply more global communications links.[20]

It is significant that in 1985 Intersputnik signed a cooperation agreement with Turner Broadcasting of the United States. Likewise it is notable that the Soviet Union has established an earth station for the sole purpose of linking into the Intelsat network.[21] This kind of interlinkage between the communist bloc and the Western democratic world is indeed becoming endemic.

As Long rightly suggests, "For more than 275 million Soviet citizens, Moscow is the political, cultural, and social center of the world," and it is likewise the hub of the country's domestic television system. The Soviet Union has 115 television production centres that produce a wealth of programmes in more than 45 languages and which are broadcast across the country's ten time zones.[22] Although the Soviet Union is so badly underdeveloped in both political and economic terms, that certainly does not apply to its broadcasting establishment.

A rather different kind of service is operated by the International Maritime Satellite Organization, or Inmarsat. The world's only major nonmilitary mobile satellite communications system, it provides a variety of services – telephone, telex, data, and facsimile transmissions, and distress and safety communications – to shipping and offshore installations and in some instances to aircraft and to users of mobile ground links.[23]

Inmarsat was established in 1979, and in its organisation it is patterned rather after Intelsat. It has 48 member countries, and from its London headquarters it operates a global satellite communications system covering all of the world's great oceans. The Inmarsat system comprises three main operating segments: ship-based earth stations, coastal earth stations, and the space satellites which link the earth stations. In addition, experiments are under way to perfect stations which will be placed on board aircraft and linked to the earth stations by means of the satellites. Likewise several manufacturers are now producing, under Inmarsat auspices, miniature earth stations which can be packed in suitcases, taken for example to earthquake or other disaster sites, and be linked directly into the Inmarsat global system.

Ever since Marconi's success in developing long-distance radio communications, it has of course been possible to link ships at sea with shore-based radio stations or with other ships. However, sunspots and other electromagnetic disturbances can cause havoc with long-distance radio broadcasts, and vital messages often become unintelligible. But communication by satellite has changed all that, and now clear and reliable messages can be exchanged with ships sailing in virtually any part of the world. In the same way, oil rigs and other marine installations have been linked into the network, and so has the airborne and hand-carried equipment just mentioned. The Inmarsat system has proved a resounding success.

In addition to the foregoing global satellite systems, our planet now possesses several thriving regional systems. One of them was created by the European Telecommunications Satellite Organization, or Eutelsat.

46

Established in 1977, Eutelsat has 25 member countries as follows: Austria, Belgium, Cyprus, Denmark, Finland, France, the Federal Republic of Germany, the United Kingdom, Greece, Holland, Iceland, Ireland, Italy, Liechtenstein, Luxembourg, Malta, Monaco, Portugal, San Marino, Spain, Sweden, Switzerland, Turkey, the Vatican City, and Yugoslavia.[24]

In the early days of Eutelsat, the planners thought that their spacecraft would mainly serve to supplement the existing European terrestial telecommunications network, but the attractions of pan-European television broadcasting soon became apparent. In addition to their conventional telecommunications uses, Eutelsat's satellites now blanket Western Europe with a wide variety of television programmes; and they are playing an important political and cultural role in helping to unite the Western European community.

In 1976 the League of Arab States established the Arabian Satellite Communications Organization, or Arabsat. Organised as a cooperative, Arabsat includes the following 21 members: Algeria, Bahrain, Djibouti, Iraq, Jordan, Kuwait, Lebanon, Libya, Mauritania, Morocco, Oman, the Palestine Liberation Organization, Qatar, Saudi Arabia, Somalia, Sudan, Syria, Tunisia, Yemen Arab Republic, People's Democratic Republic of Yemen, and the United Arab Emirates. Arabsat's transmissions pretty well blanket the Arab world and include an English-language news broadcast each day.[25]

In 1976, Indonesia – which is longer East to West than the United States and with its some 175 million people ranks as the fifth most populous country – became the fourth in the world to establish a comprehensive domestic satellite system.[26] Known as Palapa, the system has proved an enormous success in linking together that vast

47

archipelago. Palapa transmissions include television, voice, and high-speed data services for the government, the business community, and the general public. The Palapa system has meanwhile become truly regional in scope, for it also supplies television channels and other telecommunications services on behalf of Thailand, Malaysia, and Singapore. Likewise, Indonesia, together with five other Southeast Asian countries, has made an agreement with Intelsat to use Palapa satellites for operating television news services between the countries.

In addition to the fleets of civil satellites operated respectively by Intelsat, the Soviet government, and Inmarsat, and the regional systems operated by Eutelsat, Arabsat, and Palapa, numerous satellites are being put into service by other individual countries – often through private companies based in those countries. Among the countries involved with such actual or projected satellites are these: Australia, Brazil, Canada, Colombia, Federal Republic of Germany, Finland, France, India, Iran, Ireland, Israel, Italy, Japan, Luxembourg, Mexico, Norway, Papua New Guinea, Saudi Arabia, Sweden, the United Kingdom, and the United States.[27] Canada, France, and Japan, for example, are particularly active in this field; but the overwhelming majority of such civil satellites are those sent aloft under contract with the U.S. private sector, which now has a fleet of *more than fifty* such birds in space. This to a degree – but only a degree – counterbalances the Soviet Union's leadership in space.

With so many countries wanting to send satellites into space, naturally the demand has grown for additional launch capacity. Here the Soviet Union clearly leads the world; as we have seen, she annually launches about three times as many military and civil satellites as all the rest of the world put together. In part this astonishing launch rate stems from the fact that Soviet satellites tend not to remain operational as long as those built in the West;[28] but it also arises from advanced and sophisticated Soviet launch capabilities and from the high priority which the Kremlin gives to space matters both civil and military. It is no accident that, in addition to its arsenal of military space vehicles, the Soviet Union has led in creating the great Intersputnik communications system with its global reach.

Meanwhile the West, together with China and to a limited extent Japan, has been building up non-Soviet launch capacity. The United States has so far employed some ten types of launchers for satellites and other payloads.[29] Much reliance was placed on the Shuttle programme until the Challenger disaster of 1986, and subsequently the Americans decided to discontinue using the Shuttle for commercial payloads and to reserve it for scientific and military purposes. This helped to create a serious backlog of American satellites awaiting launch, and U.S. companies have therefore had to think of foreign as well as domestic launch opportunities. Because of the technological secrecy factor the Americans avoided entrusting their satellites to the Soviet Union for launch; with the People's Republic of China, however, the attitude has been somewhat more relaxed, and agreement has been reached for limited Chinese launching of U.S. satellites. Japan will in due course also be offering commercial launches.

Meanwhile the Western European Arianespace programme, which launches rockets from its equatorial site in French Guiana, has fortunately proved a great success, and more and more Western satellites are being sent aloft that way. In 1989 Arianespace signed a $3 billion contract for the procurement of 50 Ariane-4 rockets for launching satellites or other payloads;[30] this was the biggest-ever such contract and symbolised Arianespace's confidence in the West's space future.

It is well to remember that the space age, which for practical purposes began with Sputnik 1, is just over thirty years old. Yet already it has become clear that a revolution is at hand – both in global communications terms and in other terms which are both sinister and salubrious. The cultural consequences will be arresting to say the least.

4 Cultural Chaos?

In 1989, in America, a man named Ted Bundy was executed after confessing to the murder of 28 women. In a taped interview released after his death at dawn in Florida, he blamed his behaviour partly on dangerous impulses which he said "are being fuelled day in and day out in the media" in their various forms, naturally including television.[1] Ever since the world's first regular public television service was inaugurated, as we have seen, in London in 1936, a debate has continued on television's cultural impact, which many people have viewed with alarm and despondency. Not surprisingly, the advent of satellite television, and particularly of direct broadcasting by satellite, has made the debate still more lively.

Actually the debate antedated the advent of television, for the earlier inauguration of regular public radio broadcasting had likewise brought much soul-searching as to standards. Although many people have helped to formulate an ethos for what has become the global broadcasting enterprise, outstanding among them was Sir John (later Lord) Reith (1889–1971), a towering Scotsman who was in no doubt as to what he stood for. As the first General Manager and then the first Director General of the British Broadcasting Corporation, he formulated and promulgated a broadcasting philosophy which some people have found unduly austere but which has continued to provide a source of inspiration.

Asa Briggs has supplied an admirable summation of the Reithian philosophy as follows:

> Reith's theory of public service began with the conception of the public. Without such a conception the conception of public service itself becomes bleak and arid. . . . The 'publics' are treated with respect not as nameless aggregates with statistically measurable preferences, 'targets' for a programme sponsor, but as living audiences capable of growth and development. The BBC, in brief, was to be dedicated to 'the maintenance of high standards, the provision of the best and the rejection of the hurtful.' Reith had no sympathy with the view that it is the task of the broadcaster to give the customer what he wants. 'It is occasionally indicated to us that we are apparently setting out to give the public what we think they need – and not what they want – but few know what they want and very few what they need. . . . In any case it is better to overestimate the mentality of the public than to underestimate it.'[2]

Tom Burns has referred to the "moral and cultural zeal which was Reith's own personal endowment to broadcasting."[3] And the BBC Empire Service (as it was originally called), as established under Reith's leadership, was imbued with that same zeal and has become universally recognised for its integrity and reliability. The Empire Service had been Reith's brainchild, and he had fought for five years to bring it about. Finally, on 19 December 1932, the initial broadcast went out. In the high-minded words of the BBC's Chairman, J. H. Whitley, "This wireless, one of the great gifts of Providence to mankind, is a trust of which we are humble ministers. Our prayer is that nothing mean or cheap may lessen its value, and that its message may bring happiness and comfort to those who listen." Reith's own inaugural address matched the significance of the occasion. Radio, he asserted, is

> an instrument of almost incalculable importance in the social and political life of the community. Its influence will more and more be felt in the daily life of the individual in almost every sphere of human activity, in affairs national and international. . . . It has been our resolve that the great possibilities and influences of the medium should be exploited to the highest human advantage. . . . The service as a whole is dedicated to the best interests of mankind.

Very soon afterwards, on Christmas Day 1932, the new service was given a flying send-off when King George V used it to broadcast throughout the Empire. As Reith reported, "it was the most spectacular success in BBC history so far. The King has been heard all over the world with surprising clarity." And the King was "very pleased and much moved" when Reith sent him a bound volume of letters received from all over the Empire.[4]

On the scientific side a great step forward had already taken placc in the early 1920s through the work of Sir Edward Appleton, whose researches had led to the identification of ionised layers in the upper atmosphere against which short wave signals could be bounced back to earth. Reith consistently championed scientific research on broadcasting and the construction of high-powered transmitters for international work. His initiative was to prove more timely than even he could have expected.

As the 1930s wore on and the storm clouds gathered over Europe, Hitler and Mussolini proved themselves increasingly adept at harnessing international broadcasting for propaganda purposes. This presented a major challenge for the Empire Service or the BBC Overseas Service as it was re-named in 1939.[5] As early as 1935 Reith had prepared a paper, entitled "The Position of the BBC in War," in which he expounded his fundamental philosophy on the subject. Pointing out that some people thought that the BBC's prime wartime role should be to maintain civil morale, Reith took strong exception. For him what mattered most was integrity. "It is essential," he wrote, "that the responsibility and reliability of the BBC's News Service should be established beyond doubt, even though in practice accuracy could not amount to more than the nearest approach to absolute truth permitted by the overriding war conditions, including censorship."[6]

By the end of 1940 the BBC was broadcasting in 34 languages, of which 25 had been added since the war began. By the end of the war in Europe, the BBC was speaking to the world in 45 languages. Meanwhile, and especially in the face of the Nazi threat, the BBC's transmitting power had been greatly boosted. Thus, as Mansell puts it,

> the initial advantage enjoyed by the Germans at the outbreak of war . . . had been largely wiped out by the end of 1943 and the BBC's engineers were able, with increasing effectiveness, to provide the broadcasters with the

technical means to achieve that domination of Europe which Goebbels himself was eventually compelled to acknowledge.[7]

By V-E Day the BBC, in its global outreach, had achieved unparalleled success. As a parliamentary committee was later to express the matter,

The British Broadcasting Corporation emerged after the war with a unique reputation for the quality and objectivity of its programmes and with all the immense prestige derived from having been during the darkest days the voice of freedom and the prophet of victory. It was also by far the greatest national broadcasting system in the world. . . .[8]

But that predominance was soon to be challenged. From the 1950s onwards, the giants of international broadcasting — in terms of total programme hours per week — were the United States, the Soviet Union, and the Chinese People's Republic.[9] During the 1970s and 1980s, the United States and the Soviet Union have run more or less neck-and-neck at very high levels of broadcasting output, while the PRC has not been far behind. The fourth place has gone to the German Federal Republic. Again in terms of total programme hours per week of international broadcasting, Britain has run fifth.

Here, however, lies the fascinating paradox. For it is one thing to broadcast; it is quite another thing to be listened to. And the evidence indicates that, in audience terms, the BBC World Service (as it is now called) remains the world's biggest broadcaster.[10] Why should this be so?

The immediate explanation appears to be twofold. On the one hand, many international radio broadcasts are technically deficient, and in some cases they can be satisfactorily heard only in the originating studio. Britain is by no means the only country which has superior technical standards in broadcasting, but her standards have helped her to reach the largest worldwide audience. On the other hand, and perhaps even more important, many international broadcasters have largely transmitted propaganda. The BBC, by contrast, has the enviable distinction of having become known, over a period of many years, for its objectivity and reliability. People throughout the world have a way of responding to this.

But the explanation for the BBC's dominant global audience position also resides at a deeper level. Much has been said and written about so-called cultural diplomacy, which as J. M. Mitchell suggestively points out, "seeks to impress, to present a favourable image, so that diplomatic operations as a whole are facilitated."[11] In hearings before the Foreign Affairs Committee of Britain's House of Commons, John Tusa, in his role as Managing Director of the BBC World Service, opted for the term "valuable diplomacy." Using the term in the sense of "the overall presentation to the world at large of the values of British society," he commented as follows:

> These values are personal as well as political, scientific as well as artistic, private as well as public, and in everything we do . . . [the World Service represents] a society which is plural and diverse, rational, open to the free flow of thought and ideas, tolerant, democratic and responsible. It is not to say that we spend all our time broadcasting

about these values and advocating them. We are not a propaganda station. What matters more really is that our broadcasts in all languages reflect and are wholly informed by these values. . . .[12]

And he quoted with approval this statement by Charles Curran:

The BBC as an institution is the child of parliamentary democracy. And the whole concept of its establishment assumes its support for that system. I once heard one of the BBC's senior editors admit that we were biased. 'Yes,' he said, 'biased in favour of parliamentary democracy.' And he was absolutely right. That form of democracy depends on there being a plurality of opinions, on the freedom of their expression, on their public dissemination, and on the resolution, in circumstances of tolerance, of the differences of view which will then arise. . . .[13]

This, we might say, is the BBC's first "secret weapon." It wields the weapon to good effect throughout the world. Whenever people refer, as they quite properly do, to the BBC's objectivity and balance and reliability, what they really mean – whether they realise it or not – is objectivity and balance and reliability within the context of the parliamentary democratic tradition.

And here we come to a remarkable circumstance. No matter where and under what kind of system – whether an enlightened democracy or a one-party state or despotic personal rule – people live, they respond to the BBC's approach. Somehow it symbolises the sort of standard to which people naturally subscribe. And this holds true all over the world.

But the BBC also has available to it a second "secret

weapon." It is related to the first but often finds different forms of expression. It is known as human rights. Both implicitly and explicitly, the BBC subscribes to fundamental principles of human rights. And these principles carry a worldwide appeal which, to coin a phrase, is very much in tune with the global outreach of the BBC World Service.

Later in this book we shall have more to say about the widening role of human rights, but for the moment it is well to encapsulate the sort of fundamental rights which are enshrined in the Universal Declaration of Human Rights as approved in 1948 by the United Nations General Assembly without a single dissenting vote but with certain countries for obvious reasons choosing to abstain. Drafted to provide "a common standard of achievement for all people and all nations," the Universal Declaration contains 30 fundamental articles from which the following excerpts are indicative:

> All human beings are born free and equal in dignity and rights. . . . Everyone has the right to life, liberty and security of person. All are equal before the law and are entitled without any discrimination to equal protection of the law. . . . No one shall be subjected to arbitrary interference with his privacy, home or correspondence, nor to attacks upon his honour or reputation. Everyone has the right to the protection of the law against such interference or attacks.

Such rights as the above were repugnant to various regimes, especially a number of those in the communist bloc, and even more does this hold true of the following additional rights as contained in the Universal Declaration:

Everyone has the right to own property alone as well as in association with others. . . . No one shall be arbitrarily deprived of his property. . . . Everyone has the right to freedom of thought, conscience and religion. . . . Everyone has the right to freedom of opinion and expression; this right includes freedom to hold opinions without interference and to seek, receive and impart information and ideas through any media and regardless of frontiers. . . . Everyone has the right to take part in the government of his country, directly or through freely chosen representatives. . . . The will of the people shall be the basis of the authority of government; this will shall be expressed in periodic and genuine elections which shall be by universal and equal suffrage and shall be held by secret vote or by equivalent free voting procedure.[14]

In Britain the struggle for human rights of course began considerably earlier. This clause, from Magna Carta as agreed to by King John in the year 1215, is suggestive: "No free man shall be taken or imprisoned or disseised [i.e. deprived of his lands] or in any way destroyed, nor will we go upon him nor put upon him, except by the lawful judgement of his peers or the law of the land."[15] Now the point is that Britain's cumulative human rights tradition has continually interacted with her evolving tradition of parliamentary democracy; and the BBC's global audience has shown itself to be peculiarly responsive to both traditions. I believe that this goes far to explain why the BBC continues to attract such an enormous and loyal following worldwide.

It is not sufficiently realised that the BBC's international radio broadcasts have already benefitted significantly from the satellite explosion. Using two Intelsat geostationary satellites, one over the Indian Ocean and the other over the Atlantic, the BBC World Service delivers its signals to a string of relay stations on diverse parts of the globe: Cyprus, Singapore, Hong Kong, Ascension, the Seychelles, Masirah (off Oman), and Antigua. The signals reach the relay stations in what is proudly called "studio quality," and they are then rebroadcast to many millions of people. The World Service likewise employs a Eutelsat satellite whose area of impact or footprint covers the whole of Western Europe and a good deal of Eastern Europe as well. European countries receive the BBC's broadcasts by satellite in more than 20 different languages (of course including English) and rebroadcast them to their own nationals.[16]

In one sense the World Service greatly appreciates these rebroadcasts by proxy, but in another sense it has serious reservations about them. Under politically fair-weather conditions such rebroadcasts can, assuming good liaison, often reach wide audiences and as a bonus can further spread the use of the one universal language. However, such rebroadcasting removes essential control from the originating broadcaster – the World Service – and puts it in the hands of a third party. As John Corbett, the World Service's Chief Engineer, has pointed out, "The fundamental problem of broadcasting to a nation from within that nation is that it can ask you to leave – or kick you off air. That could happen in a time of crisis, which is exactly when you need to be heard."[17]

Comparable considerations apply to the assessment of fibre optic submarine cables, which to some extent can complement communications satellites. Fibre optic cables can in many instances compete commercially with satellites; and such cables can to a degree provide a

60

valuable security complement to satellites which could, as we shall see, be vulnerable to enemy action. But satellites are far superior to cable systems in terms of what is called overall connectivity capability; in other words, although branching from an undersea cable (which normally goes simply from A to B) is both difficult and expensive, a satellite can connect with an almost infinite number of ground stations within its large footprint area, and these ground stations can range all the way from very large ones to simple and widely-scattered domestic ones.[18] But fibre optic cables have a big future as a complement to satellites especially on high-volume routes.

As a good illustration of satellite adaptability, the BBC has been in direct contact with a citizen's group in Poland which has been listening to the 24-hours-a-day World Service on their own satellite receiving equipment, which is not illegal in Poland.[19] So the point of comparability is this: just as the BBC is reluctant to entrust too much of its rebroadcasting to third-party countries, so one may be reluctant to have international communications traffic depend too much upon particular countries where submarine cables happen to terminate. Satellites, which can be so easily linked with widely-dispersed ground stations, offer far more flexibility and far more frontier-leaping prowess.

Another major international broadcaster is of course the Voice of America and its affiliated stations. In one respect it and the BBC World Service had a similar genesis, for both experienced their fastest growth during the Second World War. The first VOA broadcast – in the German language – went on the air in 1942. Soon afterwards the Office of War Information or OWI was established, and the VOA became its radio division.[20]

The VOA grew very rapidly and by 1945 it was broadcasting in 41 languages.

Radio Free Europe and Radio Liberty were established as separate enterprises in 1950 and 1951 respectively. Originally they were funded mainly through the CIA, but in 1971 all connections with the CIA were officially severed. In 1973 the U.S. Congress created the Board for International Broadcasting, and its governing board now presides concurrently over both the VOA and Radio Free Europe together with Radio Liberty. Radio Free Europe broadcasts mainly to Eastern Europe other than the Soviet Union while Radio Liberty broadcasts chiefly to the Soviet Union itself.[21] The VOA also operates Radio Marti, a service especially directed to the people of Cuba, and it likewise operates a service especially designed for the people of Afghanistan.

The VOA works under strict guidelines which are contained in the so-called VOA Charter as enacted by the Congress. Among other things the Charter provides that "VOA will serve as a consistently reliable and authoritative source of news. VOA will be accurate, objective, and comprehensive." Likewise Radio Liberty/Radio Free Europe – which in terms of programme hours per week is the leading external broadcaster to the Soviet Union and Eastern Europe – operates under comprehensive and well-delineated guidelines known as "The RFE/RL Professional Code." For example, the Code specifies that the

> accuracy and reliability of information broadcast are essential to the Radios' credibility and must be beyond reproach. . . . When facts appear to be in doubt, confirmation of news items by two independent sources is required

before such items are authorized for broadcast. Editorial opinions, from whatever source, shall be clearly distinguished from news and news analysis, and the source of the opinion identified.[22]

If the VOA and its associated stations have not achieved quite the global reputation of the BBC World Service, this may be due to a complex of reasons. One is that the World Service and its predecessor services have been on the air for considerably longer than has the VOA and thus has accumulated more experience. Another is that the earlier association of Radio Free Europe/Radio Liberty with the CIA may have conjured up negative images. Still another reason is that, although both the World Service and the VOA rely upon government funding, in Britain the funding, and the associated administrative control, have operated in a slightly more indirect way than in the United States. A final reason is that, although the VOA and its associated stations have assembled a dedicated and admirably qualified staff, some of them have a State Department foreign service background which is sometimes rightly or wrongly thought to prejudice their impartiality.

Be all that as it may, the VOA has over the years achieved an enormous and generally constructive impact, and this is attested to by the sustained efforts made to jam its broadcasts. The regimes running the Soviet Union and its empire have indeed spent vast sums trying to jam Western radio broadcasts in general and those of the VOA and its associated stations in particular. They have done this in spite of the fact that each hour of jamming costs about three times as much as one hour of broadcasting.[23] It was in 1987 that Moscow stopped jamming the BBC and the VOA as such, and then at the end of 1988 Moscow ceased its jamming of Radio Free Europe and Radio Liberty. Other countries in the Soviet bloc have generally followed suit; and so, after some 40 years of largely unsuccessful effort, the Soviet Union and its associated regimes have lifted the electronic curtain against Western radio stations. The whole concept of jamming had indeed proved a political boomerang; primarily it had reacted back against the countries which had for so long attempted the jamming.[24]

The VOA has followed the BBC example in making more and more use of satellites for relaying its radio broadcasts worldwide; and in 1983 the Congress agreed to appropriate over $1 billion for a major upgrading of the VOA's engineering infrastructure including a global satellite interconnect system which is now well advanced.[25] Such satellites enable the VOA to broadcast with far greater range and fidelity than before.

In the realm of television, a further illustration of the flexibility of satellites is provided by Visnews, the world's largest television news service, which in turn forms part of the London-based Reuters, the leading global news and information agency. Reuters had of course been founded by the German Paul Julius Reuter (1816–1899), who in 1849 had used the available technology to set up a continental pigeon post; had established a news agency in London in 1851; and had then built up a worldwide news service based on the use of the telegraph. It is intriguing to reflect on the fact that the enterprise, in its infancy preoccupied with birds, today utilises latter-day birds in the shape of satellites and indeed operates the world's biggest privately-leased communications network,[26] largely based on satellites.

Visnews was the world's first agency to distribute

news daily by satellite. Its news services are used by over 400 broadcasters in some 85 countries. Visnews' coverage is seen on an estimated 470 million television receivers worldwide. It is a thrilling experience to visit the central newsroom at the Visnews London headquarters, with its global satellite interconnections and its operations running 24 hours a day and 365 days a year. Moreover, Visnews prides itself on its dedication to "the highest principles of responsible international visual journalism," which with plausibility it claims to be independent of any national or commercial interest.[27]

Moreover, a key part of the Visnews philosophy is that, far from being unilateral, it operates a television *exchange* programme with the broadcasters in all of the 85-odd countries with which it has links. This was brought home to me when, not so long ago, Visnews concluded a news exchange agreement with that Alice-in-Wonderland country Burma, which was my first overseas post and which has long been known for its relative isolation from the rest of the world. Visnews has done much to help overcome news blackouts, and its exchange arrangements with so many countries – not least with the Soviet Union and the People's Republic of China – have in the best visual sense opened many windows on the world.

An equally distinguished television news agency, and one which again is founded squarely upon satellite broadcasting, is World Television News or WTN. Based in London and New York and operating around the clock every day in the year, WTN uses satellites to distribute news worldwide – and again in both directions. Owned by three leading television organisations (ABC in America, ITN in Britain, and the Nine

Network in Australia), WTN employs a highly experienced staff who work in many countries and who seek to maintain what WTN calls "the highest international standards."[28]

It has become fashionable to think of Western radio and television as providing a diet of soap operas, quiz shows, portrayals of violence, and pornographic or quasi-pornographic films; and certainly there is no lack of such elements of doubtful nutritional value. But the cultural mix also includes other ingredients of much greater value. For example, the radio and television output of *both Eastern and Western* Europe includes many splendid offerings in such fields as music, ballet, literature, natural history, and science and technology. These carry wide appeal regardless of culture or ideology.

But perhaps the most significant cultural common denominators relate to news. The world's thirst for news is constant and unending, and this principle applies irrespective of culture or ideology or indeed geography. Moreover, people all over the world display a strange quirk: they prefer reliable news to unreliable news. The overwhelmingly positive global audience response to the BBC's World Service, for example, provides validation of the foregoing principle.

In the realm of television, audiences throughout the world have one thing in common – an almost insatiable appetite for reliable news and authentic news pictures. This again applies regardless of culture or ideology and regardless of where on Earth the viewers happen to live. The universal desire for such news and news pictures goes far to explain the ever-widening international and intercultural reach of satellite television.

Amidst what is often seen as a prevailing state of cultural chaos, we find astonishingly rational and universal human responses. We can build upon these in ways to be described later in this book.

5 Re-mapping the World

In broadcasting circles the story is told of an English woman tourist who, visiting Afghanistan during the Soviet occupation there, found herself surrounded by an angry mob who thought that she was Russian. She kept shouting, "British, British!" but nobody understood. On an impulse the terrified woman then shouted "BBC, BBC!" whereupon the mob suddenly relaxed and departed leaving her in peace.

This incident illustrates the long reach of global broadcasting and its cultural impact. In 1989, as Soviet forces were pulling out of Afghanistan in effective defeat after nine years of bloody war, Western correspondents were indeed sending live television reports from remote Afghan guerrilla bases using portable satellite uplinks. Thus were political and cultural signals conveyed through space.

The field of geography deals very largely with areal or spatial matters. As a standard source puts it, "Spatial arrangement of data is an essential characteristic of geography." Among various divisions of the field is of course social geography, which can be regarded as providing "a multifaceted perspective on the spatial organization of mankind."[1] Social geography, in short, deals very largely with spatial order and with spatial patterns of world society.

In earlier years geography dealt essentially with terrestial matters involving the surface of the Earth, but with the advent of the space age that has changed. A definitive book, entitled *Beyond Spaceship Earth*, has elucidated the extent of the change. For example, in spite of the justifiably-growing concern about Earth-bound environmental issues, man is also obliged to consider such issues in their off-planet context. Not only has man already landed on the Moon but also the Soviet Union and the United States have respectively visited Venus and Mars with unmanned spacecraft. Many of the planets have been partially or completely photographed and mapped. Man has already littered space with much debris. Plans are being drawn up to exploit the mineral and other resources of various of the planets, and some environmentalists argue that only in this way can we avoid a disastrous depletion of the resources of Earth. The time is overdue to consider the ethical and environmental dimensions of space.[2]

According to T. Stephen Cheston, "Humans have projected upon space their hopes, fears, analytic abilities, and other paraphernalia of their psyche with unending vigor." In earlier centuries, he points out, space was "wonderfully inaccessible and therefore a vent for the brimming exuberance of the human imagination." But now the space-flight revolution

has made it imperative . . . that we come to grips with the fundamental phenomenon of *the physical marriage of human culture with space.* Not to do so would condemn us to be prisoners of our unconscious predispositions, misdirecting our energies or, in the extreme case, laying the seedbed for the extinction of civilization. To do so can enrich the entire fabric of human knowledge, shine forth fresh light on old questions, and generally elevate the human condition. . . .[3]

Cheston discerns the emergence of space social science, which he calls *spaceology* and which he defines as "that branch of knowledge that treats the origin, development, and varieties of the interaction between human culture and the extraterrestial environment. Spaceology would draw upon the humanities, social sciences, and natural sciences with equal facility."[4]

What and where are the main interfaces between human culture and space? For one thing, they focus on technology created by man and launched into space. As Cheston puts it,

Be it in space or on the ground, technology is still technology and is a product of human culture. It is created in response to particular human needs, and once created it in turn affects culture. Peculiar to space technology, however, it also places people for the first time in physical environments radically different from those found on Earth. . . .[5]

Yet actually it is by no means necessary to be an astronaut or live aboard a space station in order to experience the sensation of being at the interface between human culture and space. If one travels aboard an airliner at "only" say 30,000 feet, even then one can experience something of that sensation. Moreover, one can derive the same sort of sensation from various intellectual and emotional experiences without necessarily leaving the ground at all. The use of a flight-simulator – whether designed to train pilots for "near" space missions or astronauts for deep space ones – provides an obvious example.

One of the most elegant ways of experiencing life at the interface between human culture and space is through remote sensing. One can define remote sensing as relating to the acquisition of information about distant objects. The human eye is indeed a remarkable remote sensor, and on a clear day it of course often enables one to see large objects even several miles away. But remote sensing generally refers to acquiring information through the use of instrument-carrying ships, aeroplanes, or space vehicles. For example, photography from aircraft came into extensive use as early as during the First World War, and with advancing photographic technology it has remained important to the present day. But in the remote sensing field the most exciting developments relate to the use of satellites.

Especially important among such satellites are those in the Landsat series launched by the United States. The first of these, sent aloft in 1972, originally carried the mouth-filling name Earth Resources Technology Satellite 1; but in 1975 it was re-christened as Landsat 1. As Paul J. Curran points out, "This satellite proved to be of great importance as it gave remote sensing worldwide recognition and was the harbinger of the unmanned Earth resources satellites of today."[6] Landsat 1, which was about the size of a small car and which remained in service for almost six years, generated a wealth of valuable information about our Earth. Moreover, it is important to realise that this was in the fullest sense a *communications* satellite, for it collected data from the Earth's surface and then, on an unrestricted basis, transmitted the data to distant receiving stations located on diverse parts of the globe.[7] The information garnered by Landsat 1 was truly spectacular and, to coin a phrase, it opened up a whole new world and a most colourful one at that.

Landsat 1 has been succeeded by a series of further Landsat satellites. Among other highly productive remote sensing satellites are those which have been launched by France and entitled SPOT (Satellite Probatoire d'Observation de la Terre). For example, within six weeks of its launch in 1986, SPOT 1 had transmitted images of 80 per cent of the world's capital cities. One of the advantages SPOT satellites enjoy over Landsat ones is that they can view to the side of their orbital paths; and they can also obtain stereoscopic coverage by viewing things from different angles on successive passes. Although the centre of SPOT activities is the main receiving station at Toulouse in France, receiving stations have also been established in a number of other countries.[8]

Most satellite-mounted sensors are of the so-called passive type which record radiation naturally emitted from the Earth in the form of light or thermal energy.[9] One of the interesting exceptions, however, has been Seasat, which employed a so-called active system which bounced radar signals off of the Earth. Although designed primarily for scanning the seas, Seasat proved – during its short life of 106 days in 1978 before its electrical system failed – that it could generate data for portraying such "targets" as the City of Los Angeles in remarkable detail.[10] In the future we are likely to see much more in the way of radar-carrying satellites for remote sensing.

On the other hand the Earth's natural radiation provides plenty of energy for generating a wealth of "self-portraits" through remote sensing from space. Moreover, these portraits – many of them of great beauty, as depicted, for example, in *Images of the World*[11] – can include both physical *and cultural* features of man's earthly habitat. One finds an ever-growing literature on the applications of remote sensing, and only a brief indication can be given here. For instance, during the 1960s, 1970s and 1980s the United States, the Soviet Union, and latterly Western Europe, have built up a sizable fleet of meteorological satellites.[12] These give a far more comprehensive picture than ever before of evolving global weather patterns. Increasing worries about the so-called Greenhouse Effect make the role of these satellites for climatological purposes all the more important.

Likewise the analysis, by satellite remote sensing, of global soils and land formations is of obvious and immense importance to man, who depends upon productive soils for his sustenance.[13] Again, satellite surveys of the Earth's rocks and mineral resources throw much light on prospects for development and on geopolitical factors as well. In the same way, satellite surveys can directly contribute to solving problems of ecology, conservation, and resource management. Likewise sensor-carrying satellites are extensively employed for studying crop patterns, crop yields and similar matters.[14] Remote sensing by satellite is moreover proving enormously helpful in hazard monitoring and disaster assessment, whether these relate to storms and hurricanes, insect infestation, or other conditions threatening man and his livelihood.[15]

Man has markedly influenced – not necessarily for the better – the Earth's climate along with its water and soil and mineral resources and much else; but it is when we come to the global *built* environment that his impact stands out most conspicuously. Perhaps optimistically, the United Nations has estimated that by the year 2110 the world population could stabilise at 10.5 billion, around double what it is today. As C. P. Lo has indicated, "The impact of population growth on global resources, the global environment and global development remains a major challenge to be faced by mankind."[16] And as our planet becomes ever more crowded with humans, it is they who mainly change the face of it. Beavers may dam streams and larger animals may blaze wide trails across the terrain; but it is chiefly man who has created large visible artefacts. These include railways, highways, reservoirs and much else; but it is especially man's villages, towns and urban conurbations which stand out conspicuously.

Remote sensing can provide enormous help in tracking the spatial distribution of human population and in recording the interaction of man with his environment. A combination of satellite sensing, airborne radar and aerial photography can provide amazing insights. For example, the U.S. Air Force's Defense Meteorological Satellite Program collects night-time images of villages, towns and cities and other human installations throughout the world; and among other things it has produced dramatic comprehensive images of all major cities and conurbations throughout the entire eastern half of the United States.[17] Likewise, aircraft and satellite imagery plays a valuable role in plotting present and prospective locations for agriculture, industry and transport; and it can provide a spatial inventory of atmospheric and land and water pollution.[18]

Remote sensing scans can throw much light not only on how many people are living in a given area – say the rapidly-growing capital of a developing country – but also on their socio-economic condition. It is here that we return to the relationship between human culture and space. Geography, as we have seen, deals very largely with spatial matters in the terrestial sense. But in today's world we must also consider extraterrestial space and the interaction between culture and space. This calls for imaginative thought of a high order – but not beyond the capacity of any thinking citizen who is reasonably "with it". We have now, after all, entered into the space age.

Another branch of geography is of course political geography, which after a quiescent period shows signs of coming back into its own. According to an authoritative source, "In the idiom of modern geography, geographic quality attaches to any phenomena, human as well as nonhuman, intangible as well as tangible, exhibiting *areal* dimensions and associations. . . ."[19] In geographical discourse,

> any section of the Earth's surface delineated by reference to political criteria is a political area. . . . As geographers have emphasized . . . , the 'impress' of political authority changes both the physical and social aspects of landscapes: it affects, for example, inspection stations and other boundary structures; transportation grids that conform to political requirements . . . ; movement of goods and people within a frame of migration and commercial laws; and linguistic and other cultural homogeneities imposed by political authority.[20]

What happened within the Soviet Union under Lenin and Stalin provides conspicuous examples of the "impress" of political authority, and of course the process was extended, with no little brutality, throughout the geographical area of the Soviet empire. But soon the process transcended the realm of portions of the Earth's surface, large though they might be. From the 1957 launch of Sputnik 1 onwards, the Soviet Union moved towards preeminence in the extraterrestial field, and Soviet planning has naturally included the concept of human habitations in space. As Cheston has succinctly observed,

> it can be expected that in the twenty-first century we will scale up the size of operational units in space from space stations and bases to space towns. Whether on the surface of the Moon or Mars, or floating in open space . . . , these relatively large aggregations of population will repeat in some ways Earth-based experience and, in other ways, represent something totally new. Their social mores will be determined in large degree by their sponsoring entity. It is one thing to be in a moon base controlled by the Soviet military and another to be in a floating space colony founded by the Quakers. . . .[21]

Although extraterrestrial geography (as distinguished from astronomy) and spaceology are still in their infancy, we have available to us a number of useful indicators. As J. P. Cole points out, there are two elementary facts which affect the whole of the surface of the Earth: "places differ from each other in various ways, and each place is uniquely located in relation to all other places." And he refers to the Earth as a place where some 200 countries share hundreds of international boundaries of greatly varying length.[22] According to Peter J. Taylor, "In the current world-economy the crucial events that structure our lives occur on a global scale." And he observes that "Three geopolitical regions have developed new world powers – Japan, China and [Western] Europe – to join the USA and the USSR."[23] It should be noted that all five of Taylor's geopolitical regions *have likewise become space powers*.

With the exception, points out Richard Muir, "of inhospitable polar regions and a few scattered areas where colonial relationships survive, the land surface of the Earth is now divided up into a patchwork of sovereign states."[24] These states, he suggests, are *the behaviour units* in an international system composed of states, their colonies and protectorates, and international organisations. And he conveniently classifies the Earth's states into the two super-powers; China as a near-superpower; Japan, the United Kingdom, and other great powers; a group of lesser powers; and assorted minipowers. (The European Community, although not a state as such, clearly has the makings of a superpower.) "The fundamental actors in the international system," he notes, "are sovereign states, and the main motive force directing their behaviour is the pursuit of the 'national interest' of each as it is perceived by the decision-makers composing the various . . . governments."[25]

At the moment – and many people would say that this is a blessing – we have no parallel extraterrestial sovereignty system, but we do have something slightly akin to it. With the Soviet Union as presently the dominant space power, Soviet leaders naturally think that they have a vested interest in space, whether for military or civil purposes. In spite of treaties or conventions, and in spite of fine talk about space being reserved in perpetuity for peaceful purposes, the Russians will increasingly seek to exercise a kind of qualified sovereignty in

77

space. Particularly where they have space stations or space colonies, they will seek to defend them against all intruders. The United States and other space powers will show similar responses. Moreover, as we shall see, even space vehicles such as unmanned satellites cannot be guaranteed to be safe from molestation, and this potential danger can in turn provoke counter-measures.

Meanwhile it is no accident that the Soviet Union is among world leaders in its use of space for global broadcasting, and this brings us to the whole matter of cultural geography. According to a standard definition, cultural geography in the broad sense "deals with any part of man's culture in the same way that plant geography deals with the distribution of plant species and vegetation or that economic geography is concerned with the production and distribution of goods and services."[26] Cultural geography relates to the diffusion of cultures and culture traits over space and time. The meaning of space in this context has been undergoing rapid change; not too many years ago one took it for granted that the space concept referred to terrestial space and to spatial diffusion on the surface of our Earth, but that is no longer necessarily the case. Since man has extended his influence and his presence into extra-terrestial space, cultural diffusion has extended into that realm as well.

It was Marshall McLuhan who, in a book first published in 1964, propounded the celebrated thesis that "the medium is the message."[27] He was of course referring primarily to the terrestial electronic media of his day, and his argument was widely criticised as simplistic. With the dramatic subsequent growth of man's extraterrestial activities, and with communication

78

having acquired new spatial dimensions, one might be tempted to revive the McLuhan thesis; but that would be a mistake. A sounder philosophy would be that dramatised by the BBC during World War II, when it eventually triumphed over the Nazis both in broadcasting power and in the basic solidity of the content of the message.

In 1956, the year before Sputnik 1 heralded the advent of the space age, two eminent Harvard scholars, Carl J. Friedrich and Zbigniew Brzezinski, published a book on totalitarian dictatorship and autocracy which, with reference to Soviet and other totalitarian regimes, concluded with the thought that "large portions of mankind" may have to pass through the totalitarian crucible, "before becoming ready, if they survive the ordeal, for more complex forms of political organization."[28] (By more complex they of course meant more complex and enlightened, such as democracy.) More than three decades later, in 1989, Brzezinski published a sequel work with the resounding title: *The Grand Failure: The Birth and Death of Communism in the Twentieth Century.*[29] Much had happened to the world between the publication dates of the two volumes, and many lessons had been learned. We shall return to some of the themes of Brzezinski's book in due course.

Meanwhile, in 1988, a work entitled *Capitalism, Communism and Coexistence*,[30] was published under the authorship of John K. Galbraith in collaboration with Stanislav Menshikov, a staff member of the *World Marxist Review* and former high-ranking Soviet government official. The work helps to make clear the remarkable degree of convergence as between Soviet intellectuals and those of the West. Terms such as the free market, formerly despised in Soviet circles, now

win approbation. Soviet economic and political thinking, even if not necessarily Soviet practice, is increasingly meeting that of the West more than half way.

But the process goes much further. All over the
world – with notable interim exceptions such as China,
North Korea, and others that can be identified –
governing regimes are moving towards an acceptance
of the mixed economy concept. Likewise they are
getting the message that it is no longer prudent to give
the appearance of ignoring human rights. In these
respects sophistication is growing and horizons are
widening.

In 1974 (with a second edition in 1986), a delightful
and pioneering little book, by Peter Gould and Rodney
White, was published under the simple title *Mental
Maps*.[31] All of us retain mental images of places with
which we are familiar or somewhat familiar. For example, the authors display a most engaging map showing a
native New Yorker's idea of the United States of
America, graded according to relative familiarity.
Brooklyn and the other parts of New York City are
enormous, and New York State covers a major part of
the entire country, with all the rest regarded as hinter-
land. In the same way one can draw mental maps of the
spatial images of citizens of diverse other countries,
often with astonishing results. Muir, Haggett, and
others have elaborated on this same kind of suggestive
thinking.[32]

Needless to say, we can visualise mental maps not
only in the idiom of spatial geography but also in terms
of the *intellectual* landscape. Thus it is not uncommon to
say that somebody is blinkered or provincial in his
thinking. Yet I knew a Vermont farmer, a rugged
individualist, who cheerfully admitted that he had

never travelled outside of his home county; "but my mind," he said, "has wandered a great deal." On the other hand Gould and White cite the case of a young girl who had just returned from a salubrious holiday in Majorca. Asked where Majorca is, she replied that she didn't really know – she had gone there by plane.[33]

According to a fundamental principle in the field of political culture, "In all dynamic political systems, tensions are possible because the socialization process cannot change as rapidly as the political process."[34] "Socialization" in this context of course means the process of the cultural assimilation of change. And this brings us straight back to the fundamental problem faced by Gorbachev and his successors in trying to push through reforms.

John Lloyd has posed the following question:

> ...The ending of the 'class war' as the foundation of foreign policy; the reduction of 500,000 troops, and real measures to scale down activity and tension in the Far East, Southern Africa and Afghanistan; the intent to introduce contested elections to a new full-time parliament; the liberalisation of journalism, publishing, academic life and travel; the encouragement of market relations throughout industry and the countryside – can all these and the hectic pace at which they are being driven through an inert or even hostile bureaucracy by the reformers, be any less than real?

Lloyd indicates that he is "pretty much convinced" by this line of reasoning; but he cautions that some leading Soviet political activists take a quite different position which does not lack plausibility. The reforms, they argue, cannot be really genuine unless and until the

81

Soviet leadership takes the one decisive step: the ending of one-party rule.[35] And the leadership has shown little inclination to do this, although conceivably the leadership might bring in such a fundamental reform by stages and by indirection.

Where has Gorbachev obtained his support against the bureaucracy with its privileges and its vested interest in perpetuating the status quo? According to Menshikov, he received general support "from the Party; from a large part of the population, particularly the workers in the enterprises; from the farmers who need more freedom to run their farms; and much support from the intelligentsia, especially the creative intelligentsia, by which I mean the literary and artistic world, the press, the media in general."[36]

In Menshikov's interpretation, "For the first time since the Soviet Union was established, it has been replacing the very foundations of socialist society."[37] When we recall the above-mentioned fundamental principle of political culture, we see inevitable major difficulties in the process of the cultural assimilation of change. In the Soviet case the situation has been exacerbated by the fact that, at least initially, the reforms have brought worsening shortages of consumer goods and an actual decline in the standard of living.[38] Menshikov, along with Gorbachev and many others, has grossly underestimated the obstacles to the assimilation of change.

Menshikov, himself a Marxist, estimates that about one third of the world's people live under socialism while capitalism encompasses two thirds.[39] He argues that his own country, the Soviet Union, must take drastic steps towards freer markets and a freer society. And by implication he believes that *all* of the socialist countries should achieve the benefits which he recommends for his native land. The Soviet Union, after all, has from the beginning considered itself to be in the vanguard of the so-called socialist camp, and it must not surrender that leadership role. If some people were to argue that some countries in the socialist camp already operate a system of democratic socialism, Menshikov would logically reply so much the better – that is what we want for them all, and the Soviet Union can lead the way.

George Bush and other Western leaders have repeatedly warned that the Gorbachev phenomenon – not to mention Gorbachev himself – might collapse at any time and that it would be most imprudent to mount a massive Western programme of aid to the Soviet Union along the lines, say, of the Marshall Plan. But the French have long had a category of aid which can suit the situation very nicely. It is called intellectual aid, and it stems from the French rational tradition going back to Descartes (1596–1650)[40] and before. Although intellectual aid is by nature intangible, it can prove most powerful. Intellectual aid can, moreover, be related to mental and intellectual maps.

Some people have criticised the concept of intellectual aid because they think it smacks of arrogance. But, considered properly, this need not be so at all. In the context in which we are considering the matter, the giving of intellectual aid might better be called a simple matter of enlightened self-interest – and a gesture of goodwill as well. In addition, intellectual aid, unlike material aid, need in no way deplete the donor's resources. In fact, the reverse is the case, because intellectual aid not only regenerates itself but leads directly to fresh insights and a broader and deeper body of knowledge. In the best conservationist sense, intellectual aid is a renewable resource.

Every region of the world has cultural values and expertise to offer to every other region. But if we compare the prevailing situation of the Soviet Union and its empire – not to mention a variety of other countries in the so-called socialist camp – with that in Western Europe or North America or Japan, we see a vast contrast. Here, if there ever was one, lies an enormous opportunity for the transfer of values and expertise to places where they are desperately needed. The transfer process can make full use, in ways which we shall be further examining, of the frontier-leaping capabilities of contemporary communications technology. A global perestroika is taking shape. We are in the process of re-mapping the whole world.

6 Combined Space Strategy

As Boris Yeltsin swept to overwhelming victory in his Moscow constituency in the Soviet general election of March 1989 – the first such general election since Lenin's seizure of power some 70 years before – he clearly stated where in his view perestroika had come unstuck. "I think where the tactics of perestroika went wrong," he said, "was in not starting with problems which everyone would have understood: food, goods, and living conditions. We had this grand declaration of 'perestroika on a large front' but we simply do not have the resources nor the finances for such a large front."

Yeltsin added that, for the sake of expediting the fulfilment of perestroika, "we need to hold up the space programme for five to seven years."[1] Declaring that three-and-a-half years had already been wasted since the promulgation of perestroika, he called for a new emphasis on priorities for the people.

Much of what Yeltsin said had the ring of plausibility. But a major moratorium in the Soviet Union's massive space programme seemed unlikely, if only because space had become so much a part of the Soviet cultural context. For example, in a book on Soviet space achievements published as early as 1959, Ari Sternfeld hailed the launching of the Earth's first artificial satellites as "a great victory for Soviet science and technology in the peaceful competition between the two systems of capitalism and socialism." He declared that the victory "was won thanks to the diligent organized labor of Soviet scientists, engineers and workers and to the unprecedented growth of science and technology in our country during the years of Soviet power."[2]

In the view of G. I. Pokrovsky, a leading Soviet space engineer, writing at the same time,

> The creation of an intercontinental rocket and its use for launching . . . artificial earth satellites is a very great victory for the science and technology of our Soviet fatherland. Representatives of Soviet aviation are especially glad to acknowledge this. Indeed the mighty new rocket technology grew up predominantly on the basis of Soviet aviation culture.

And he went on to refer quite frankly to the "combat power of intercontinental missiles" – the same sort used to launch the satellites – and their ability to strike targets in any part of the world. Such power, he explained, "substantially enlarged the possibilities of modern military technology" and it "singularly strengthens our armed forces."[3]

This leads directly to the nub of the dilemma over space technology. Ironically the planet Earth's first artificial satellites – i.e., the initial Soviet ones – were launched as a component part of the programme of the 1957–1958 International Geophysical Year, and the Soviet achievement was justly hailed as a contribution to scientific knowledge. But already it had become apparent that the satellites, and the rockets used to propel

86

them into orbit, had the most far-reaching defensive and offensive military implications. Now, well over three decades after the launch of Sputnik 1, it requires little imagination to discern that the traditional concept of the commanding heights now refers in large measure to space.

Yet, unless it is carefully and fully understood, such a concept can amount to an oversimplification; for, as we shall see, "commanding heights" in the space age refers to ideological and cultural considerations as well as to military ones. It is very important to grasp the fascinating complexity of man's use of space.

As Christopher Lee has succinctly observed, "Space is now dominated by the needs of the military." Space technology, he adds,

> has promised to give the solution to so many of the traditional problems of the military commander that governments have had no option but to press onwards and upwards, until today it can be shown that about three-quarters of all satellites are used by the military. Space is now the eyes, ears and the voice of the modern military commander. Yet this is but the beginning.[4]

Space, as Gordon Robson has observed, has taken on a chameleon-like quality.[5] In similar vein William E. Burrows has referred to the particular field of remote sensing as "an ambiguous undertaking."

> When it is conducted in order to measure forestland, inventory wheat production, or track schools of tuna, it is called resource management. But when the same cameras are turned on submarine construction facilities at Groton or Severomorsk, or on ballistic missile complexes in South

Dakota or Svobodnyy, it becomes [military] reconnaissance. . . .[6]

Rip Bulkeley and Graham Spinardi, referring to the 75 per cent of all satellites used for military roles, note that these naturally fall under several major headings including (1) reconnaissance, (2) communications, and (3) navigation; moreover, meteorological and geodetic surveying satellites, although seemingly "scientific" in nature, are also important for military purposes. Military *reconnaissance* satellites divide into five different categories as follows: photographic; electronic intelligence; ocean surveillance; early-warning; and nuclear explosion detection. Of all military satellites launched by the United States, the Soviet Union, and China, about 40 per cent have been used for photographic reconnaissance from low Earth orbit (between 200 and 5000 kilometres above the Earth's surface), and some of these are thought to be able to discern objects less than 30 centimetres across.[7] Military photographic reconnaissance satellites also travel in a variety of other orbits.

Electronic intelligence satellites are equipped to monitor military, diplomatic and other radio communications. They can pick up the microwave pulses emitted by the ship-defence radars of other navies, and they can "trawl" from space to obtain a whole variety of Soviet or other communications signals. Ocean-reconnaissance satellites can locate ships and take other maritime measurements at all times and in all weathers. Early-warning satellites carry infrared detectors which can provide the superpowers or other powers with warnings of incoming missiles. Satellites for detecting nuclear explosions can be used to help enforce nuclear test-ban and non-proliferation treaties; and paradoxically they could also prove very valuable in prosecuting nuclear war.[8]

The same paradoxical quality attaches to the field of *communications* satellites, which so readily lend themselves to military as well as to peaceful purposes. The military establishments of both the Soviet Union and the United States, particularly the latter – and America's allies as well – depend upon satellites for a wide range of military communications, and as we have seen they have indeed become a mainstay of the modern military commander. At the same time the famous Washington-Moscow "Hot Line," which has perceptibly helped to avoid superpower misunderstandings, has been carried by satellite since 1978.

Military *navigational* satellites, as distinguished from ocean-reconnaissance ones, permit much more accurate navigation of warships in general and of nuclear-missile submarines in particular. It is essential for such submarines to know their exact location at sea in order to fire their nuclear missiles with precision, and this is what navigational satellites enable them to do. Likewise so-called scientific satellites, including meteorological and geodetic ones, can greatly facilitate military planning and operations by providing information on weather, on the Earth's geographical features, on its gravitational and magnetic fields (which affect the accuracy of long-range missiles) and the like.[9]

For many years there have been wistful and wishful statements about reserving space for the purposes of peace, but meanwhile the major military powers have been busy seizing the commanding heights. As Kirby and Robson conclude in their book on *The Militarisation of Space*, "The age of space militarisation has arrived and it is probably too late to prevent it, though the pace

89

at which it happens can possibly be altered."[10] This assessment appears to be a balanced one and it is nowhere better illustrated than by what has happened in the field of anti-satellite weapons or asats.

Earlier the Russians had displayed an almost pathological distaste for unauthorised overflights of their territory whether by plane or satellite, and both in the United Nations and otherwise they had vociferously objected to such flights. But then, particularly after the Americans publicly revealed some of their spectacular remote sensing images, the Russians changed their tune; they decided that they wanted to be in on the act, and they vigorously set about developing their own equipment. As Stares notes, "By the time the Soviets withdrew their objections to 'espionage satellites' in the UN in September 1963, they had already launched *nine* low resolution reconnaissance satellites." Other higher resolution ones were soon to follow.

The changed Soviet posture may well have been prompted in part by the Cuban missile crisis of 1962, when the world seemed on the brink of war and when remote sensing had played a key role in exposing Khrushchev's Cuban gamble. Both superpowers had been chastened by that experience and both had come to realise that co-operation might be better than confrontation. President Kennedy helped the Russians to save face when he declared a blackout on the publication of U.S. satellite overflight data. This no doubt reduced the Soviet incentive to try to shoot down American satellites, but it certainly did not remove that temptation.

Having become aware of how vital satellite data had become for military strategy and tactics, each side inevitably turned its attention to finding ways of dealing with the other's military satellites – and possibly civil satellites as well. The natural temptation to develop antisatellite weapons, or asats, is well illustrated by the scenario painted by John Hackett and others in their book entitled *The Third World War*. In their scenario,

> Active hostilities opened first of all . . . with widespread and clearly very carefully prepared attacks on U.S. communications and surveillance satellites. The Soviet interference capability was known to have developed considerably. . . . The extent of its development came as an unpleasant surprise. . . .[12]

Soviet asat development seems to have started about 1963, and by 1968 they had successfully tested their ground-based orbital interceptor. Carried aloft by a powerful rocket and equipped with a radar sensor and a pellet-type warhead, the interceptor can attack any satellite operating at an altitude of up to 5000 kilometres or more.

According to *Soviet Military Power*, a standard U.S. government source, as of 1988 the Soviet Union had *the world's only operational asat system*. They had built many orbital interceptors and they had a wide range of rockets to carry them aloft, together with all the infrastructure needed to complete the system. In addition the Russians have been doing much research on the use of lasers to attack military or civil satellites and on means of damaging them through high-powered electronic interference.[13]

Although the Americans have developed asat techniques which are commonly regarded as superior to those of the Russians, stop-go responses by the Congress and by successive administrations have meant that the United States has no proper operational asat system. The main U.S. system consists of a homing vehicle mounted on a small two-stage rocket which is carried aloft aboard a fighter plane to a height of about 20 kilometres and then fired. The homing device, which is known as a Miniature Homing Vehicle or MHV, is guided to its target by its internal computer, infrared sensors, and small sideways gas thrusters which can correct its trajectory. No explosive warhead is needed since the vehicle destroys its target by direct collision at high speed.[14] The system, while promising, is obviously of little practical use unless it is carried beyond the prototype stage and deployed. The United States is likewise researching asat possibilities entailing the use of lasers or electronic interference.

The whole subject of asat weapons is greatly complicated by their intimate technological relationship to nuclear ballistic missiles and means of defence against them. Many criticisms have been made, by concerned scientists and others, of the Strategic Defense Initiative or SDI or "Star Wars" programme as first announced by former President Ronald Reagan in 1983 and as carried over in modified form by President George Bush. Whereas the programme was originally billed as designed to provide a "leakproof umbrella" to prevent nuclear missiles from reaching the soil of America or her allies,[15] latterly the tendency has been to concede that such an anti-ballistic missile or ABM umbrella could never be entirely leakproof. This made some critics all the more vociferous, for they were able to argue, with some plausibility, that even one or a few non-intercepted intercontinental nuclear missiles would wreak such havoc as to render the whole defence exercise meaningless. The United States SDI programme has of course

92

likewise been roundly condemned by the Soviet leadership.

What many Western critics have overlooked is that the Soviet Union already has the *the world's only operational ABM system,* on which it has expended far more in manpower and other resources than has the United States on its still-formative system. The Soviet research effort has especially concentrated on high-energy lasers, on particle beam and kinetic energy weapons, and on radio-frequency weapons which can interfere with or destroy the electronic components of incoming ballistic missile warheads. In addition the Soviet Union has overwhelmingly surpassed the West in the field of passive defence against nuclear missiles. According to *Soviet Military Power,*

> The Soviet passive defense program is a comprehensive system of measures designed to inhibit the effects of a nuclear attack on the Soviet Union. The main objectives of the passive defense program in effect today are: ensuring the survival and continuity of the Soviet leadership; planning for efficient wartime mobilization of manpower and the economy; protecting the industrial base and essential workers; and providing a credible reconstruction capability. Integral to the Soviet passive defense program are thousands of hardened facilities.[16]

For the past 40 years the Soviet Union has been implementing a vast programme designed to ensure leadership survival in the event of nuclear war. This has included the construction of deep underground bunkers plus tunnels, secret subway lines, and other facilities beneath Moscow as well as other major Soviet cities and the sites of key military commands. These underground facilities are in some cases hundreds of metres deep and can accommodate thousands of people.[17] Construction of these facilities continued in the 1980s in spite of the Soviet peace offensive. The West has nothing to match them nor any early possibility of such.

Now for present purposes our concern is not primarily with the vast Soviet missile defence programme as such but rather with its relationship to global communications strategy. And here we find a paradoxical situation indeed. As Barnaby aptly expresses it, "Antisatellite warfare and ballistic missile defence are very closely related – Siamese twins, so to speak. This is so because of the need to protect the space assets – including satellites, space battle stations, mirrors, and so on – which are so crucial to ballistic missile defence as it is now often envisaged."[18] Once such assets are deployed, the other side will make plans to attack them, and these plans will in turn rely on satellites. Thus a circular situation will develop wherein the satellites required for any effective defence against incoming ballistic missiles will in turn become subject to attack using information obtained from other satellites – all of this contributing to general chaos in space.

The situation is complicated still further by the fact that any defensive weapon designed to neutralise incoming enemy missiles or their warheads can also be used as an offensive weapon to attack the enemy's satellites. For example, the Soviet Navy operates the world's largest strategic missile submarine force, and the Soviet Air Force operates the world's largest and heaviest missile-carrying bombers;[19] and these forces rely upon military satellites for guidance. With the distinction between defensive and offensive space weapons so effectively blurred, Soviet commanders could be forgiven for thinking that "defensive" anti-missile weapons were in fact intended for offensive use with the aim of destroying the satellites which serve as the commanders' eyes and ears and voices.

Many people have, for good and proper reasons, pleaded for the conclusion of a treaty to ban or limit antisatellite weapons, and discussions on a possible asat treaty actually took place between the United States and the Soviet Union in the late 1970s.[20] But the United States broke off the discussions in response to the Soviet invasion of Afghanistan at the end of 1979, and they were not renewed. The complicated interrelationships between asats and other kinds of space weapons may in any case make this a lost cause, and one of the contentions of this book is that other more tension-reducing and peace-fostering avenues exist. Meanwhile it appears certain that asats are here to stay and that they will be further developed and made more lethal and more menacing as the years go by.

Moreover it is highly unlikely, Gorbachevism notwithstanding, that the Soviet Union will dismantle its operational anti-ballistic missile system or its operational antisatellite weapons system or its vast civil defence infrastructure. This being the case, it becomes incumbent upon the United States, in collaboration with its allies, to develop parallel but more advanced operational systems as a matter of overriding urgency. This will be no easy task, particularly in view of political inertia in some Western centres of power and influence; but the integrity of the Western partners demands it.

Any attack on military or civil satellites would, according to some experts, instantly be regarded as an act of war. But with modern laser and electronic techniques it may well be possible surreptitiously to

95

degrade satellites while giving the impression that they have become inoperative through some internal defect. World leaders have meanwhile become more and more aware of the ideological and cultural power, as well as the military potency, of communications and other satellites. It has not been lost upon such leaders that, in the context of advanced communications, knowledge is power. It is not for nothing that Hackett and colleagues, in their scenario of a Third World War, describe measures to wreck enemy communications satellites and portray the use of manned orbiting spacecraft to disseminate propaganda in enemy territory.[21] It is not just in the conduct of war that satellites and other space vehicles can play a crucial role, but also in the *prevention* of war.

Although civil and military satellites must be defended by military means if necessary, paradoxically the best satellite defence lies with the *messages* conveyed by the communications satellites themselves. This concept, far from being abstract and abstruse, can be expressed and implemented in very practical terms. It involves the use of satellites to spread a kind of global glasnost which enhances the safety both of the satellites and of mankind in general. When, for example, President Gorbachev has used international satellite linkages to proclaim the virtues of perestroika and even of some limited reliance upon the Western-style market economy, that helps to establish common denominators with the West. If, on the other hand, worldwide satellite-carried television reports that the KGB has brutally put down a nationalist demonstration in one of the Soviet republics, that serves as a warning to the Soviet leadership that they are acting contrary to accepted international norms. Satellites having contributed

96

mightily to the creation of a one-world information system, that system in turn contributes to a one-world social situation.

Researchers in the United States, the Soviet Union and other countries are working to "harden" communications and other satellites to make them less vulnerable to military attack. As we have intimated, however, the best form of protection for communications satellites — and by implication for other kinds of satellites as well — lies in the *content* of the pictures and messages which the satellites convey. These signals can in practice help to establish a global cultural climate which is safe both for satellites and for civilised society.

Bhupendra Jasani and colleagues have, in their book on the subject, argued persuasively for the use of satellites for arms control and crisis monitoring and for thus giving such satellites a major additional peacekeeping role. As Jasani suggests in this pioneering work,

> Observations from satellites offer a unique opportunity for the verification of compliance with international agreements and for the monitoring of crises throughout the world, mainly because of their non-intrusive nature. Whereas the most advanced technology for reconnaissance from outer space is classified, because it is used on board military satellites, the level of detail and accuracy in remote sensing by civilian satellites has in recent years increased to the extent that a new potential emerges for international co-operation in the verification of arms control treaties and in crisis monitoring. . . .[22]

Although, as the book points out, an obvious approach to this matter would be through the creation of a United Nations-sponsored satellite monitoring agency, the Soviet Union and the United States oppose such an idea because it would infringe on their quasi-monopoly of military satellite data. As a next best, Jasani and colleagues propose the establishment of a European regional satellite monitoring agency to be sponsored by the European Economic Community or another suitable body; and they suggest that another parallel monitoring agency might be set up for the Asia and Pacific region.[23] Using satellites owned or leased by them, these regional agencies could keep a close watch on adherence to arms control treaty provisions and on crisis situations.

Another alternative would be for a dedicated quasi-private organisation such as the Washington-based United States Institute of Peace or the Stockholm International Peace Research Institute to sponsor such satellite monitoring in aid of peace. It could in turn contract with one of the new breed of companies (e.g., the Spot Image Corporation of Reston, Virginia or the Earth Observation Satellite Company of Landover, Maryland) which, as Burrows points out, are already engaged in large-scale high-quality global satellite sensing on a commercial basis.[24] With such a demonstration of effective satellite monitoring, and with the presumed further spread of the spirit of glasnost, Moscow and Washington might then end their resistance to the creation of a UN-affiliated global satellite monitoring agency set up in conformity with the UN's declared aims.

It is a perennial precept in the field of international relations that that subject has to do with power – even though nobody has ever fully defined exactly what power means in that context. As F. S. Northedge indicates in his *The International Political System*, "The possession of power is, and must be, the normal indispensable condition for the attainment of whatever goals a state sets for itself in the international system, and for the defence of any interests and values it deems to be important. . . .[25] The historian Paul Kennedy, in his massive study entitled *The Rise and Fall of the Great Powers*, concludes that "To be a Great Power – by definition, a state capable of holding its own against any other nation . . . – demands a flourishing economic base."[26] This, he explains, provides the essential basis of durable military clout. Joseph Frankel, in a suggestive analysis, regards state power as "a potential for influence." Power, he points out, "has, in fact, been the necessary condition of self-preservation, and a state which ignores this condition cannot escape the danger of disappearing. . . ."[27] And in an especially salient passage he states as follows:

> . . . Although power does play a central role in international politics, it is fundamentally an instrument for the achievement of national values. International politics is determined not only by the power wielded by the various states but also by the values held by these states; the concept of 'national interest' which governs state behaviour is not limited to power considerations alone.[28]

The place of power in the modern world is very well exemplified by the role of the Soviet armed forces. In Brian Moynahan's carefully-researched book *The Claws of the Bear: A History of the Soviet Armed Forces from 1917 to the Present*, he characterises the Red Army (his shorthand for the Soviet armed forces) as "the world's most powerful institution."[29] With more than five million men in its ranks (not to mention more than eleven

99

million reservists), it is, for example, well over double the size of the U.S. armed forces. With its enormous submarine fleet (including the world's largest individual subs), it has some of its submarines permanently on station just off the U.S. East coast, from which a single missile could vaporise Washington, D.C. within five minutes of the order to fire having been given. The Soviet armed forces have vast resources, and in important categories vast superiority over NATO, in the contemporary paraphernalia of war. The Soviet military's all-pervasive satellite fleets girdle the earth.

Officially the Soviet armed forces are under the firm control of the Party, and Gorbachev seems determined to maintain the Party's ascendency. The Red Army represents an enormous and prestigious establishment ensconced in the middle of a backward civilian economy, which Gorbachev is bending all efforts to improve. "Until it happens," Moynahan suggests, "and it will be immensely difficult, Gorbachev remains in hock to senior officers." In important respects, as we have noted, Gorbachev's efforts parallel the earlier ones of Krushchev; and Moynahan reminds us that the October 1964 coup against Khrushchev was supported by the military.[30]

In the Soviet Union, according to Moynahan,

the military are the only consumers who are taken seriously. The defence ministry has its own huge complex of 'closed' factories which work only to its orders. Where it shares a plant with a civilian production line, the products are made to a different standard and under rigorous quality control. Military quality is better than export quality. The domestic consumer gets the . . . junk.

100

The Soviet military economy, he adds, is the one sector of the overall economy "that has performed brilliantly."[31] In his view, "The Red Army, not the Party, is the superpower."[32]

That superpower, whether defined as the army or the country, has a global reach and a global outlook. Moreover, in the modern era, as Gregory C. Radabaugh of the U.S. Air Force has noted, "the Soviet Union has stated that victory in any terrestrial conflict cannot be achieved without control of space. . . ."[33] It must be remembered, adds John L. Piotrowski as Commander in Chief, North American Aerospace Command and United States Space Command, "that Soviet space war-fighting doctrine is an integral component of overall military doctrine. Soviet doctrine does not view space as a separate theater of miltary operations but as an extension of the terrestrial environment. . . ."[34]

That same Soviet doctrine can well be applied to military and nonmilitary matters alike. An obvious linkage exists between what we can call the three Ps: Power, Persuasion and Peace. In the 1990s and beyond, it is essential for the West to safeguard the inviolability of its fleets of communications and other satellites which it can employ to spread the cause of free speech and human rights throughout the world. And it is equally essential to use those satellites in the spirit of emerging global glasnost for building a structure of durable peace. It is for these purposes that we can fashion the combined space strategy.

7 The Cross-Cultural Consensus

In 1989 a British company struck gold in Japan: it introduced Western-style fish fingers. The Japanese, renowned for their fastidiously-prepared traditional fish dishes, nevertheless embraced fish fingers with unbridled enthusiasm. One of course notices, as one travels about the world, plenty of other pervasive, even if often seemingly superficial, symbols of Western culture. Indeed one finds it difficult to escape from such Western artifacts as hamburgers, Kentucky Fried Chicken, Coca-Cola, and certain items of apparel – not to mention the ubiquitous Western pop music and videos including so-called wall-to-wall "Dallas." Such artifacts are commonly associated with various kinds of moral and social permissiveness – and not just among the young.

It is often maintained that such artifacts as the foregoing represent merely a kind of cultural veneer and that they should not be allowed to obscure deeper Western cultural trends and values. Clearly there is an element of truth in this, but it should not be reduced to simplistic form. For example, some people contend that what a woman wears is unimportant – it is what is inside that matters. It has long been recognized, however, that feminine apparel provides a very sensitive social barometer and one that indeed helps to distinguish one cultural epoch from another and one contemporary society from another. Moreover, it is not at all uncommon for a woman to state candidly that the way she dresses can profoundly affect her psychologically.[1]

Various aspects of contemporary Western culture have of course been widely criticized not only within the West itself but even more so in other parts of the world. For example, Indonesia, as the fifth most populous country (after mainland China, India, the Soviet Union, and the United States) and the one which contains the world's largest Islamic community, provides a particularly good case study of the dilemma of Westernization. The Indonesian leadership, who symbolize moderate Islam and who are dead set against any proposal to create an Islamic state, have drawn highly valuable cautionary lessons from the recent tragedy of Iran.

Iran's 1978–79 revolution carried profound implications for all Islamic communities and for the world at large. According to Sir Anthony Parsons, Britain's ambassador to Iran in the most turbulent period of that revolution, "the scale of the political earthquake . . . was equal to, if it did not surpass, that of the two great revolutions of modern European history, the French and the Russian." But he adds that what took place was actually not so much a revolution as a counter-revolution – and one that effectively meant retrogression to the sociopolitical structure of more than half a century before. In Parson's opinion, many of those who took part in, or acquiesced in, that counter-revolution "must now be filled with boundless regret."[2] As Amir Taheri cogently puts it, all "thoughts, ideas, doctrines and philosophies that are not squarely based on Islam" are regarded by Iranian fundamentalists as dangerous to Islam; and this includes "almost the whole of Western political experience, and it is in this sense that fundamentalist Islam rejects the West."[3]

It is often forgotten that Iran's Shah Mohammed Reza Pahlavi had long been recognized as a devout Muslim and that the Ayotallah Khomeini could scarcely claim superiority in this respect. It is true that in Iran there was considerable corruption, which reached even to certain of the Shah's close relatives. It is likewise true that some political prisoners received torture that was thoroughly cruel, inhumane, and unjustified no matter the nature of their offences; in reporting on Iran in 1978, however, Amnesty International indicated that such torture appeared to be on the decrease,[4] and in any event it paled in scope and savagery compared to what was to follow under Khomeini. Although a degree of corruption and of torture represented two important shortcomings under the Shah's regime, in my judgement two other kinds of policy defects contributed much more to bringing on the revolution.

One of these fundamental policy mistakes concerned economic growth. The Shah's father, Reza Shah, had done much to transform Iran into a modern state, and his son was determined to follow in his father's footsteps. He had a profound conviction that only through rapid economic growth could modern – chiefly Western – amenities be put within the reach of the people at large, and he worked day and night in his zeal to achieve such growth. In successive years Iran did in fact attain some of the world's highest growth rates; and then, in the early 1970s, came the quadrupling of world oil prices with vast cash benefits for oil-rich Iran, and this prompted the Shah to order a still further acceleration of the national development programme.

Under such pressure, existing logistical and other bottlenecks worsened and fresh ones appeared; but this was not the main point. The Shah and his economic advisers had tragically failed to take into proper consideration *the cultural side-effects* of rapid economic growth. The cultural problem, already serious before the acceleration, became even worse after it. Big Western-style capital-intensive projects had been largely favoured, and increasingly the ordinary Iranian felt like a bystander in his own country. Western films and the uncritical emulation of Western ways, particularly by the young, proved deeply disturbing to Iranians who cherished the values of their own traditional culture.

The fourth major policy mistake was if anything even more serious than the third one. The Shah was thoroughly devoted to modern – i.e., largely Western – education, and with a truly religious fervour he sought to bring it to all of his people. He rapidly expanded elementary education, he organized a pioneering Literacy Corps under which soldiers went to teach in the villages, and he lavished countless millions of dollars on building up the system of high schools, technical schools and colleges, and universities. During those years, moreover, the Shah sent more students for training abroad – mainly of course to the West – than did any other Middle Eastern leader.[5]

The Shah, in his zeal to modernize his country with utmost speed, gave an unstinting welcome to Western technology and to all the paraphernalia of what has so rapidly become the world science-based culture. People with religious sensibilities – mainstream moderates as

105

well as the more fanatical elements – watched with horror as the country's own ancient culture became increasingly inundated with Western films and television programmes, pop music carried by cheap transistor radios to the remotest corners of that large country (over twice as big as Texas), and Western curricular concepts. They were aghast to see girl students reduced to promiscuity on the fine new university campuses and to witness the dissolution of family traditions and the rapid rise of divorce. Thus the Shah unwittingly played into the hands of the extremists, who soon unleashed a revolution.[6]

The ensuing decade witnessed almost unbelievable retrogression. The war with Iraq was a disaster. The regime's human rights record was a disaster. The economy was in a state of disaster. Culturally the country atrophied. Iran's strained relations with the Western world were somehow epitomized when, in a Friday prayer meeting in 1989, Hojatoleslam Ali Akbar Hashemi Rafsanjani, the Speaker of Iran's Majlis or Parliament and subsequently the country's President, publicly advocated (and characteristically later denied that he had advocated) that Iranians should kill British, French and American citizens in revenge for Palestinian casualties in territories occupied by Israel. He urged that five such Western citizens should be assassinated for every "martyred" Palestinian.[7]

His recommendation caused suitable outrage in the West and led to a general tightening of security precautions and demands for a joint condemnation by the major Western powers. But the revolution's fervour had by no means yet spent itself, nor had its capacity to foster international terrorism or to export its revolutionary doctrines. Among countries deeply concerned

106

about such Islamic fundamentalism was of course the adjoining Soviet Union. According to Taheri,

> In 1927 no more than 11.5 per cent of the total population of the USSR were Muslims; in 1986 Muslims were estimated to represent nearly 18 per cent of the population, or a total of 53 million. This made the USSR the sixth largest 'Muslim' country in the world after Indonesia, Nigeria, Bangladesh, India and Pakistan. Population trends established in the 1980s showed that by the year 2000 Muslims could well number more than 80 million or some 26 per cent of the total population of the USSR, while true Russians would represent no more than 22 per cent. The Soviet Union is therefore faced with a Muslim problem both within and beyond its borders.[8]

Dilip Diro points out that the Iranians have been regularly beaming radio broadcasts to the six southern Soviet republics where most of the Soviet Union's Moslems live.[9] Shaul Bakhash notes that Iran has built a new transmitter near the Soviet border to augment broadcasts into the southern Soviet republics.[10]

Uncritical Westernization very largely led to the Iranian Revolution of 1978–79. Likewise the Russian Revolution of 1917 – or more particularly its ensuing totalitarian Leninist expression – arose very largely from uncritical Westernization in the shape of the indiscriminate application of Western Marxism. In the face of ever-increasing adversities the Iranian Revolution had still not lost its zeal; but the same could not be said for the Russian Revolution. Reference has already been made in Chapter 5 to Zbigniew Brzezinski's *The Grand Failure*, and it eloquently describes the evolving disintegration of what he calls the Soviet system and dogma. Although the following references in no way do full justice to his analysis, they serve to relate it constructively to our present theme.

Since Brzezinski has a rather mouth-filling name – just as I do – I shall here refer to him as *ZB*. Much of the twentieth century, he points out early in his book, "came to be dominated not only by ideological passions but, more specifically, by a passion masquerading as scientific reason, namely communism. . . ." ZB then makes the important observation that the rise of communism

> as the major political manifestation of the twentieth century has to be seen in tandem with the rise of fascism and nazism. In fact, communism, fascism, and nazism were generically related, historically linked, and politically quite similar. They were all responses to the traumas of the industrial age, to the appearance of millions of rootless, first-generation industrial workers, to the inequities of early capitalism, and to the newly acute sense of class hatred bred by these conditions. World War I brought about the collapse of existing values and of the political order in Tsarist Russia and in Imperial Germany. It generated acute social tensions as well in newly industrialized Italy. All these gave rise to movements that wrapped the concept of social justice around a message of social hatred and that proclaimed organized state violence as the instrument of social redemption.[11]

ZB notes that "Hitler was an avid student of the political practices initiated both by Lenin and by Mussolini"; and in particular "Hitler learned from Lenin how to construct a state based on terror, complete with its elaborate secret police apparatus, its reliance on the concept of group culpability in dispensing justice, and its orchestrated show trials."

Fascism and nazism were at least temporarily eclipsed in the Second World War; and now we have arrived at what ZB characterizes as the terminal crisis of contemporary communism. In his observation, "The precipitating cause of the agony of communism is the failure of the Soviet experience."[12] That experience of course effectively began with Lenin, and it was under him that mass terror "became an administrative device to solve all problems." Lenin created the system that in turn created Stalinism and made possible the crimes of Stalin. For Stalin and his cohorts, "the infliction of death on countless thousands of alleged 'enemies of the people' was a minor bureaucratic act"; and ZB regards it as "absolutely safe" to estimate the total number of Stalin's victims at no less than twenty million and perhaps as high as forty million.[13]

In 1945, when Stalin conquered Berlin, the Red Army was the largest military force in the world. By the 1960s Soviet leaders were confidently proclaiming that the Soviet Union would soon become the world's leading economic power as well; but then in the 1970s the economy became sluggish and has remained so ever since. In the 1980s Gorbachev frankly recognised that his country required a new political culture if it was to advance economically and socially. The obstacles to this were formidable; they extended back into Tsarist times but they centred on the system imposed by Lenin. It is not surprising that after seventy years under such a system, the shaping of a new Soviet political culture would require "a major political upheaval."[14]

Here ZB makes an absolutely fundamental statement as follows: ". . . Leninism and not reform was thus the

109

ultimate – but hidden – issue of contention among the top Soviet leaders. . . ."[15] We have seen, in Chapter 1, how Gorbachev has fallen over himself to eulogize Lenin; and some of Gorbachev's hardline rivals, such as Ligachev, are if anything even more wedded to Lenin. Yet a reformed Soviet political culture would be *totally alien to Lenin's whole theory and practice*.

Leninism remains central to the legitimacy of the Soviet ruling elite. In the Soviet Union it has now become acceptable, even fashionable, to repudiate Stalinism; but the public repudiation of Leninism is a much more risky matter – even though it and Stalinism are so closely linked. As ZB points out, the Soviet leadership, including Gorbachev, realize that "to repudiate Leninism entirely and openly would mean delegitimizing the Soviet system itself." ZB plausibly concludes that the political obstacles to any fundamental perestroika are "probably insurmountable."[16]

As we saw in Chapter 1, Soviet scholarship is already beginning publicly to cast doubt on Leninism, and eventually a Soviet *political* leader or leaders will have the courage to do so too. As ZB remarks, in the 1920s the communist experiment in the Soviet Union was widely regarded as promising the future; in the 1930s it seemed to be building that future; and even on into the 1960s it looked to many people like the wave of the future. "Yet," he points out, "by the waning years of this century the Soviet Union has come to be seen as an ideologically unattractive example of arrested social and economic development." Indeed, he observes, "For the world at large, the Soviet experience . . . is henceforth not to be imitated but avoided. As a result, communism no longer has a practical model for others to emulate."[17]

110

It was not only outside of the Soviet Union that people generally had acquired a jaundiced view of the prospects for communism; the same thing was happening with the Soviet citizenry as well. ZB recalls Khrushchev's 1958 boast that by 1970, if not sooner, "the USSR will have captured first place in the world both in absolute volume of production and per capita production, which will ensure the world's highest standard of living." ZB notes that the present Soviet leadership, faced with economic stagnation and a widening economic gap between their country and the United States as well as other Western powers, make no such boasts.

Meanwhile, and facilitated by glasnost, the facade of Soviet national unity had cracked. "Suppressed national aspirations and national antagonisms surfaced rapidly among the several truly historic nations of the Soviet Union, thereby belying the claim that these 'nationalities' had become submerged in a larger sense of Soviet nationalism." ZB points out that national disturbances, some on a massive scale, have lately occurred in nine of the fifteen non-Russian Soviet republics. As he sees it, "To decentralize a state-owned economy, one has to decentralize politically as well; but to decentralize the political system of a multinational empire means yielding power to previously subordinate nations." That would in effect mean turning the Soviet Union into a confederation, and it would be tantamount to the dissolution of the empire. ZB doubts whether the Russian political elite would sacrifice the empire for the sake of economic decentralization and efficiency.[18]

ZB attaches great importance to the rise in Poland of Solidarity, which has brought "the emergence of a de facto alternative political elite and the associated rebirth of genuine political life in Poland. . . ." He says this

111

rebirth "represented for communism in Poland a shattering defeat." Of particular significance was the establishment in 1986 of a Polish opposition journal especially dedicated to promoting international *regional* opposition to communist rule. Its interests include not only Eastern European countries which are under Soviet colonial rule but also various of the adjoining Soviet republics themselves. As ZB points out, "the Soviet leadership could hardly tolerate the spread of the Polish contagion to the adjoining East European states. That prospect would pose nothing less than a mortal danger to the cohesion of the Soviet empire itself." Yet the contagion has already spread further, for 1988 saw the first joint statements of the democratic opposition from Poland, Hungary, Czechoslovakia, and East Germany, calling for democracy in their countries.[19]

ZB discerns what he calls the fatal flaw in the Soviet-imposed systems of Eastern Europe. "That fatal flaw is the communist party's monopoly of power, and its root cause is Soviet domination. Forty years after the imposition of communism in Eastern Europe, the elimination of *both* is now widely seen as the necessary precondition of social rebirth." This statement is no mere exhortation but rather reflects the actual trend of events.

ZB detects a rather different trend of events in mainland China, where he finds an evolution into what he calls commercial communism. Chinese business acumen is being progressively blended with communist dogma. From 1966 to the mid-1970s, China experienced a series of brutal purges and mass killings comparable to the worst years of Stalinism; but more recently she has moved towards a doctrinal flexibility which has led to increased involvement in international

112

commerce and diplomacy.[21] One could argue that the current Sino-Soviet rapprochement tendency might enhance the Soviet regime's viability through an infusion of the Chinese commercial instinct via "the back door."

The Chinese example notwithstanding, ZB discerns "the approaching end of communism as a significant world phenomenon"; and he notes that some Soviet commentators are themselves coming to this conclusion and publicly stating as much. As a Western European symptomatic indicator, suggests ZB,

> The collapse of the communist mystique among . . . French intellectuals has contributed to the general decline in the appeal of Marxism in France. Once the dominant school of thought in the academy, in the French salons, and on the intellectually vibrant Left Bank, Marxism by the late 1970s had come to be viewed by those who shape the currents of French thought as largely passé and banal. Its place has been taken by a fascination with the implications for society of new techniques of communications and the processes not only of pluralistic democracy but even of free enterprise. . . .[22]

Although communism has gained a foothold in various of the Third World developing countries, according to ZB it has proved "a systemic failure in all of them," whether in Asia, Africa or Latin America. It is indeed difficult to think of any successful exceptions. Communism was simply found wanting in the developing countries, and by the late 1970s the Soviet model was rapidly losing its credibility. A further source of discouragement for communism lay in such examples as Angola, Cuba and Nicaragua where even massive

113

amounts of Soviet aid failed to achieve viable economies.

The communist phenomenon, in the opinion of ZB, "represents a historical tragedy. Born out of an impatient idealism that rejected the injustice of the status quo, it sought a better and more humane society – but produced mass oppression. . . . It . . . captivated some of the brightest minds and some of the most idealistic hearts – yet it prompted some of the worst crimes of this or any century." Communism indeed represented "the most extravagant and wasteful experiment in social engineering ever attempted." Fundamental to communism's failure were its philosophical roots. "Marxist-Leninist policies were derived from a basic misjudgement of history and from a fatal misconception of human nature." In the last analysis, then, communism's failure is an *intellectual* failure.[23]

With the communist system and dogma now globally discredited, what will happen next – particularly in the Soviet Union as the first major Marxist state? ZB suggests a web of related possibilities: a long-running systemic crisis with no real resolution of problems and with increasing social turbulence; renewed stagnation coupled with renewed attempts to exert central control from Moscow; a coup by the military and the KGB accompanied by emotional appeals to Great Russian nationalism; the actual overt overthrow of the Soviet communist regime; the breakup of the Soviet empire. These possibilities might interact with each other in any of a variety of ways. Although ZB suggests certain probabilities, he wisely refrains from making any flat predictions – not least because what the West does or fails to do could so materially affect the outcome.

For a superpower to remain in continuing turmoil

can be a very dangerous thing. Moreover, although one can heartily welcome the worldwide waning of communism, that can leave the planet with a highly dangerous ideological vacuum. One still finds vestiges of fascism or nazism in various countries including the United States, West Germany, and South Africa. Likewise one finds examples of ideological/religious fanaticism in certain countries including Libya and of course most conspicuously Iran. As communism progressively shrivels, other creeds are likely to appear or reappear. Certain of these might potentially prove as dangerous, nationally or even internationally, as the communism which they supersede.

In any event we can be certain of this: in one way or another, *the ideological vacuum will be filled*. We can likewise be sure that it will *not* be filled through naive Western pragmatism. Many Westerners have fallen into the habit of glibly using the "pragmatic" label without having any idea of where it came from or what it actually means. The term pragmatism was first used by the American philosopher C. S. Peirce in 1878. Peirce did not at all intend that the word should signify a viable philosophical position; but William James, John Dewey and others borrowed and distorted the term and gave it the flavour of a full-blown philosophy. In due course, as J. O. Urmson points out, the word became "a name for any position which lays emphasis on results as a test for satisfactoriness."[24]

In its corrupted and popularized form, pragmatism thus came to mean judging any proposed course of action by the following simple rule: it is good if it works. But what about successfully robbing a bank in order to solve one's financial problems, and what about courses of action that might "work" in the short term but prove ruinous in the longer term? Practical pragmatists have tended to sidestep such esoteric considerations and to opt for what have struck them as uncomplicated common-sense notions of what "works."

As Morton White suggests in his *Pragmatism and the American Mind*, pragmatism became "the most distinctive American philosophical movement,"[25] and in contagious fashion it spread into the popular culture. American politicians, business executives and others felt complimented – when they might better have felt insulted – upon being called good pragmatists. To modify Marx, one might say that pragmatism rather than religion became the opiate of the people. Why?

In earlier days in America, the practical trial-and-error approach had seemed well suited to the needs of a relatively simple technology and society, but even then it had been tempered by the strong religious impulses of the time. With the approach of the twenty-first century, however, one finds a very different situation. The pragmatic outlook readily leads into the intellectual trap *of trying to operate without any valid guiding principles*. Being a good pragmatist often amounts to being guilty of short-termism and opportunism and a failure to grasp the wider and longer-term implications of what one is doing.

Being pragmatic commonly means being simplistic. It means resorting to the technique implied in a popular but highly dangerous and booby-trapped phrase: *deciding each case on its merits*. The technique readily leads to unplanned or ill-planned responses to problems and short-sighted decisions on domestic and foreign affairs. It easily translates into such disasters as the Bay of Pigs, Vietnam, and Chernobyl.

In the absence of guiding principles, then, one

naturally falls back upon sheer expediency. Fortunately, however, the West has at its disposal a whole set of valid guiding principles which it can deploy in its dealings with waning communism or with other forms of extremism whether of the left or right. These principles indeed constitute an ever-widening consensus. That enlarging consensus has been well and concisely identified by ZB as follows: "The elevation of the State was giving way almost everywhere to the elevation of the individual, of human rights, of personal initiative, and even of private enterprise."[26]

As Seweryn Bialer and Michael Mandelbaum point out in their *The Global Rivals*,

> The political prominence of human rights owes a great deal . . . to postwar changes in the means of communication. Television has made a difference. The victims of human rights violations now have faces as well as names that are broadcast around the world.[27]

They add that "Soviet policies on . . . human rights have moved perceptibly, if slowly and unevenly, toward Western standards. . . ." And they forecast that improved Soviet official attitudes towards human rights "will probably go hand in hand with a radical expansion of the human rights struggle within the Soviet Union and with a much greater and more detailed flow of information to the West about Soviet violations. . . ."[28]

The historian J. M. Roberts, in his definitive *The Triumph of the West*, points out that

> . . . Western values and assumptions *have been internalised* to a remarkable degree in almost every other major culture. The United Nations . . . is built on the legal fiction

117

that nation states are equal, sovereign individuals. That is a western concept, fully comprehensible only within the history of western legal and political thinking, but the world takes it for granted. Or take equality, the dominant social ideal of the age, and a western one; it is in the West that the historical debate about its means and realisation . . . has taken place. . . .[29]

As ZB emphasises, the terminal crisis of communism is rendered all the more dramatic because its onset has come so suddenly.[30] We indeed live at an historic juncture in the affairs of man and woman. As the consensus steadily widens in favour of something much better than communism, we have the privilege of taking part in the articulation and long-range communication of that broadening consensus. We should waste no time.

8 Communicating the Consensus

It could well be called China's collective cry for freedom. For some five weeks in 1989, students in Beijing and many other Chinese cities staged massive demonstrations – the biggest since the communists took power four decades before – in defiance of the authorities. They demanded free speech and democracy as they saw it. In due course they met abject defeat at the hands of a brutal and reactionary clique – but their time would come.

The students and their allies obtained access, however briefly, to both the national and international communications media. People all over China, and throughout most of the rest of the world as well, soon became aware of the students and their cause; and messages of moral support arrived from far and wide. In America, at Stanford University and the University of California at Berkeley, Chinese students developed a novel use for the facsimile or fax machine – which of course works happily in any language. The students managed to collect fax numbers for machines in hotels and other business establishments in diverse parts of China. They then prepared reliable new summaries and faxed them to many places in that vast country with its approximately one billion people.[1]

Although the students and their supporters were in the first instance roundly defeated, they had made history and they knew it. Whereas an earlier generation of students had drawn their inspiration from Mao Tse-tung's Little Red Book, these students were largely inspired by the West. Many thousands of them had studied in the West, and they and their colleagues increasingly kept in touch with the West through the global media. Intellectually far ahead of the party stalwarts, the students could clearly discern the outlines of the gathering global consensus.

As the 1989 demonstrations unfolded, the reactionaries, as part of their crackdown, called for tighter ideological control of the country. An extraordinary meeting of the standing committee of the Communist Party's Central Advisory Commission issued the following statement: "This chaos has not come about by itself. One of the reasons is that we have relaxed Marxist-Leninist education for a period of time and weakened the party's ideological work."[2] Evidently the custodians of party orthodoxy – oblivious to the winds of change throughout the world – wanted to see much more communication of Marxist-Leninist principles and praxis to the population at large; and this raises the whole question of the nature of communication.

According to an authoritative source, "A broad definition of 'communication' is any transmission of signs, signals, or symbols between persons."[3] Having accepted such a plausible definition, however, we immediately encounter a fundamental fact: these signs or signals or symbols may convey information that is reliable, partly reliable, or thoroughly unreliable. If we wish to be at all sophisticated about the communication process, we have to consider the whole matter of disinformation and deception.

As Edward Jay Epstein points out in his brilliant book on the subject,

> The word 'disinformation' was in fact coined by the German High Command (OKW) during World War I. . . . Whereas deception had always been part of German military tactics at the field level, *the development of the radio forced these tactical deceptions to be centrally co-ordinated.* The OKW thus set up a special unit, called the Disinformation Service, to coordinate the forged radio traffic that was likely to be intercepted by British, French and Russian intelligence. . . .[4]

After having proved their effectiveness, especially in disrupting the Russian war effort against Germany, the German deception staff in April 1917 launched what Epstein rightly calls one of the most successful pieces of planned subversion in modern history. German military intelligence arranged a special sealed train which took Lenin and his accomplices from Switzerland, where they had been in exile, to the Russian border, where they were smuggled in and immediately began to disrupt the Russian war effort. Within a year, Lenin had seized supreme power in what had now become the Soviet Union.

Lenin received substantial German help, both in money and in intelligence, in consumating his coup. Moreover, he was not slow to learn the disinformation and deception techniques employed by the Germans. Although Germany's Disinformation Service was officially disbanded after the war, its officers and its methods played a major role in mounting a gigantic subterfuge, code-named "Operation Kama," which paradoxically took place mainly in the Soviet Union and with Lenin's connivance. Designed to evade the arms prohibitions in the Versailles Treaty, the programme, as secretly agreed to by Lenin in 1921 and continued until 1933, included the construction of German munitions plants and training facilities in the Soviet Union in exchange for German industrial equipment and patents.[5] Thus Lenin was unwittingly helping to pave the way for the rise of Hitler and his dictatorship and also for the notorious later agreement between Hitler and Stalin.

Hitler's own deception planners adopted a chilling technique to help bring about that agreement. Knowing that Stalin was paranoid about possible plots to overthrow him, they arranged to feed the Soviet security services with credible disinformation which would persuade Stalin that there was indeed such a conspiracy.[6] This was one of the factors which led Stalin to launch his massive purge of the Soviet armed forces. As Anthony Read and David Fisher point out in their carefully-researched book *The Deadly Embrace*,

> . . . most reliable estimates place the number of men who were either shot or sent to labour camps at around 35,000. At least half of the army's entire officer strength was removed, including three out of five marshals, thirteen out of fifteen army commanders, 220 out of 406 brigade commanders, seventy-five of the eighty members of the supreme military council, including every single commander of a military district, and all eleven vice-commissars of war. The remnants were inexperienced, disorganised and completely demoralised, and the modernisation programmes, which had been progressing well, were utterly shattered.

122

When it came to the question of whether he should accede to the proposed mutual non-aggression pact of 1939, Stalin, as the authors point out, had little or no choice, "for while Hitler had made Nazi Germany the best-equipped, most efficient and most feared military power in the world, Stalin himself had all but destroyed the Red Army as an effective fighting force. . . ."[7] The pact of course helped pave the way to Hitler's launching, in 1941 against the Soviet Union, of the greatest military operation in world history and one which would require four years finally to repulse.

Disinformation again played a significant role when it came to the Allied invasion of the Continent in World War II. As Epstein aptly expresses it, the Allied strategy "was to put all its eggs in one basket" and land a million men on the Normandy beaches on and after D-Day. To avoid disaster, however, Hitler and his generals had to be given a false picture of where and when the troops would land and their strategic objectives. The deception plan aimed at making the Nazis believe, even after the projected Normandy landings, that another and larger Allied force stood poised to land on the beaches of Pas de Calais in northern France. British deception planners had begun work three years earlier on planting an illusionary picture in the minds of Hitler and his high command. The deception plan comprised many elements including, for example, the creation of an entirely fictitious Fourth U.S. Army Group commanded by General George Patton and stationed in the north of England. The deceivers provided German aerial photographers with fake tanks, planes, landing craft and the like in northern England, and they put out a constant stream of phony radio messages seemingly coming from where the fictitious army group was

123

located. They concocted false announcements and stories concerning the officers and men in the huge non-existent force.

Of great assistance to the Allied deception planners was the fact that their intelligence community had cracked the German military code. As Ronald Lewin points out in his fascinating account entitled *Ultra Goes to War*, from the 1920s until VE-Day the German military had employed a sophisticated ciphering machine, known as Enigma, for secret military communications. During World War II the Germans built around 100,000 Enigma machines which they considered impregnable to code-breaking.[8] The breaking, by Britain's Code & Cipher School, of the German Enigma ciphers had a profound effect on both the conduct and the outcome of World War II.

Being in possession of the broken German code greatly strengthened the hand of the Allied deception planners as D-Day approached, since it enabled them to operate what Epstein aptly terms *the deception loop*. For it is one thing to put out disinformation and then to wonder how the enemy will interpret it; it is quite another thing to know exactly how the enemy is in fact interpreting it. The Allied deception planners were able, through their colleagues' code-breaking prowess, to obtain a constant stream of decoded messages emanating from the Nazi high command and from their field commanders. This gave the Allied deception planners complete control over the situation, for they could constantly retune and readjust their outgoing disinformation in the light of the enemy's mental state. It is no exaggeration to say that, in the events leading up to the final defeat of Hitler, the deception planners and their colleagues saved countless thousands of Allied lives and no doubt – by shortening what became the victorious campaign – a great many German lives as well.

Government-inspired deception and disinformation programmes are, needless to say, by no means confined to war situations. All of the major powers, and most of the minor ones as well, engage in espionage in times both of war and of peace, and deception and disinformation activities form a normal part of such espionage. But some countries can become unacceptably aggressive in their espionage activities, and this has particularly applied to the Soviet Union during most of its history. When, for example, a major Anglo-Soviet spy row broke out in 1989, a correspondent raised this question: ". . . Is Moscow's large-scale espionage just an anachronism . . . not yet tackled by the leadership? Or is President Gorbachev the smile that hides the KGB's fist?" The evidence suggested that, soon after he came to power in 1985, Gorbachev had given orders to the KGB and the GRU (Soviet military intelligence) to create what became a major new structure, employing more than 15,000 people and specifically designed to steal Western technology. It appeared that Gorbachev had decided that only by stealing Western technological secrets on a vast scale could he hope to make perestroika work; in effect it was a case of spying for perestroika.[10]

Epstein carries his theme much further. Although the United States and the Soviet Union have sometimes fought each other by proxy, he believes that at least through the 1990s there is no prospect of either a nuclear war or a conventional war between them. Instead there will be a conflict such as Lenin envisioned: a deception war. "In such a conflict," Epstein suggests, "adversaries can be expected to constantly attempt through peaceful means to disrupt each other's economic and military alliances, misdirect each other's energy on chimerical projects, and undermine each other's moral authority."[11] It will be a case of winning or losing without war-fighting.

At this point it is well to consider the concept of propaganda. According to a standard source, "Propaganda is the relatively deliberate manipulation, by means of symbols (words, gestures, flags, images, monuments, music, etc.), of other people's thoughts or actions with respect to beliefs, values and behaviours. . . ." There is also the related concept of "propaganda of the deed." For example, when the U.S. Air Force dropped the nuclear bomb on Hiroshima, the main objective was to help persuade Japan to surrender. Propaganda of the deed can likewise take the form of constructive demonstration projects, for instance in the field of agriculture.[12]

Propaganda, then, is an aspect of communications. Moreover, the term has honourable antecedents, for it seems to stem from *Congregatio de Propaganda Fide*, the college founded by Pope Gregory XV in 1622 for the propagation of the faith, with particular reference to teaching missions. Then, by extension, as J. M. Mitchell notes, "the word came to mean, in a sense first recorded in 1842 by the *Oxford English Dictionary*, 'Any association, systematic scheme, or concerted movement for the propagation of a particular doctrine or practice.'"[13] Although the word later acquired a more derogatory connotation, we should remember that propaganda has often served highly meritorious causes; for a single example, William Wilberforce (1759–1833) mounted very effective propaganda in the battle against slavery.

126

On the other hand propaganda can admittedly contain large elements of disinformation or deception. Paradoxically, such propaganda can deceive those who disseminate it just as much as those to whom it is directed. For example, according to Mack Smith, writing of Mussolini and his regime, "Propaganda was not only the method by which fascist leaders deceived the population in general, but also the way in which they deceived one another and the Duce himself."[14]

Propaganda techniques have, needless to say, developed considerably since Mussolini's time. As Walter F. Hahn has expressed the matter,

> Today, the . . . revolution in communications has given the propaganda weapon both extended range (that is, intercontinental dimensions) and the multiplier of the 'echoing' effect within the target society. This revolution has also dramatically raised the stakes of propaganda warfare. It is not only a generalized process of persuasion and deception aimed at target societies but also a 'precision-guided' process to penetrate to the heart of a nation's policy mechanism. It can be targeted over time to effect changes in its public mind-set. . . .[15]

Related to propaganda, but considerably more benign in its present-day connotations, is of course the concept of cultural diplomacy, which we touched upon in Chapter 4. A related concept, which has come into wide use particularly in the United States, is that of *public diplomacy*. According to Mark Blitz's convenient definition, public diplomacy "is the open civic education of citizens of other countries using means that are not deliberately false. The point of public diplomacy is primarily political (although it often uses nonpolitical methods), and there is nothing knowingly false in what it does (although which facts should be emphasized, when, and where is a matter of judgement). . . ." American public diplomacy tends to have two primary objectives. One is to inform foreign citizens about U.S. policies and their background and to encourage trust in America and her policies. The other is to inform foreign citizens about the American way of life, especially as it has been shaped by the U.S. form of government, and to foster a general appreciation of that way of life.[16]

One of the virtues of public diplomacy, especially as it is manifested in the American experience, is that it emphasizes the role of non-governmental groups and individuals. Whereas totalitarian regimes character-istically tend to monopolize the media, U.S. public diplomacy does the opposite. The emphasis on non-governmental activity and on individualism is particu-larly fitting since it harmonizes so well with the whole thrust of American political philosophy and very largely that of the West in general. As Blitz aptly points out,

> the public activity of private citizens – their voting, judging, and deliberating – is probably the most characteristic American phenomenon and the most instructive theme of public diplomacy. The work of elected representatives is similar to the public activity of private citizens. Displaying this activity is crucial to properly presenting our way of life.[17]

"Perhaps the greatest strength," adds Michael Joyce in similar vein, "in the U.S. private sector is the healthy competition of ideas, with many different centers of authority and opinion vigorously debating American purposes. . . ."[18]

128

Public diplomacy has been flowering largely because of the dramatic recent advances in global communications. As Bernard Roshco has pointed out, the new technology has even "forced mainstream diplomacy to go public."[19] Although seasoned statesmen would never concede that there no longer remains any place for private or even highly secret traditional-style diplomacy, the fact that the world may be watching frequently gives pause to leaders with totalitarian tendencies. In cases of human rights violations, for example, maximum exposure and publicity coupled with strong diplomatic pressure often provides the most efficacious remedy. Indeed, one can go further and say that a fitting response to Soviet glasnost lies in the West's own openness with a global reach.

In terms of the overall role of disinformation and deception, we can conclude that in certain spheres and at certain times – e.g., during the events leading up to the 1944 Allied invasion – disinformation and deception can have an important and proper role to play. But in most situations the truth proves much more effective – not just as a matter of short-term pragmatic expediency but durably and cumulatively. This principle is eminently valid in broadcasting, as experience with the BBC Overseas Service amply shows. Yet at the same time one should study the broadcasting strategy and tactics of authoritarian regimes in diverse parts of the world. One should take careful note of how *they* may employ disinformation and deception especially in their news broadcasting. This knowledge can help to give truth-broadcasting all the more impact. In a sense it can be like breaking the Enigma code all over again.

In the conduct of public diplomacy, or in the communication process in general, the nature and role of language is obviously of key importance. As Robert Burchfield points out, "no languageless human society has ever been discovered" on this Earth.[20] Ideally the unity of the nations would seem to imply a linguistic unity, and this brings to mind a Biblical passage in the shape of Genesis 10–11. It appears that, after the Flood, the descendants of Noah spread abroad and founded diverse nations. At that time all the nations had a single unified language. Then various of the descendants decided to build a fine new city including a huge tower – probably a so-called ziggurat – with its top in the heavens. The Lord, having come down to see the city, and having evidently decided that the people were getting above themselves, decided to take action accordingly. The Lord said,

'Behold, they are one people, and they have all one language; and this is only the beginning of what they will do; and nothing that they propose to do will now be impossible for them. Come, let us go down, and there confuse their language that they may not understand one another's speech.' So the Lord scattered them abroad from there over the face of all the earth, and they left off building the city. Therefore its name was called Babel, because there the Lord confused the language of all the earth. . . .[21]

The Lord's penalty has been a long-lasting one, for the confusion of languages has complicated global communications ever since. For example, as we have seen, the BBC World Service, the Voice of America, and Radio Moscow understandably feel obliged to broadcast in a wide diversity of languages. Many of these languages – French and Spanish, to take but two of numerous illustrations – are beautiful ones; but the quest naturally continues for a greater degree of global linguistic unity.

Although the same two illustrative languages are spoken very widely over the face of the Earth, it is English which increasingly serves as the linguistic common denominator. Anybody who has travelled widely can testify that wherever he goes he is likely to find people who speak English, and as the years go by this becomes ever more apparent. In the same way, and in percentage terms, more and more scientific papers, books, computer programmes, and musical lyrics are published in English. It is English which has become the preeminent multinational language.

As Simeon Potter points out, "The variety of its . . . vocabulary makes English more, and not less, adaptable as a medium of world communication. English now has the richest vocabulary in the world, over two hundred thousand words, apart from compounds and derivatives, being in current use."[22] According to Robert McCrum, William Cran and Robert MacNeil in their definitive *The Story of English*, ". . . English at the end of the twentieth century is more widely scattered, more widely spoken and written, than any other language has ever been. It has become *the* language of the planet, the first truly global language." English, they add, "has a few rivals, but no equals." For example,

. . . Three-quarters of the world's mail, and its telexes and cables, are in English. So are more than half the world's technical and scientific periodicals: it is the language of technology from Silicon Valley to Shanghai. English is the medium for 80 per cent of the information stored in the world's computers. Nearly half of all business deals in

131

Europe are conducted in English. It is the language of sports and glamour: the official language of the Olympics and the Miss Universe competition. English is the official voice of the air, of the sea, and of Christianity: it is the ecumenical language of the World Council of Churches. Five of the largest broadcasting companies in the world . . . transmit in English. . . .[23]

English has now become "a global language with a supra-national momentum." Apart from the many millions of people who are native English-speakers, "English is now everyone's second language, and has a life of its own in totally non-English situations." Many is the time that I have stayed in hotels in the Middle East or the Far East or Africa and have noted that guests from the Continent of Europe or from Latin America, for example, have perforce spoken only in English to the hotel staff or to local government officials or businessmen or academics. English is indeed the pre-eminent cross-cultural language.

Scientists the world over find it easier to get along with each other when they know English.[24] According to Robert Burchfield, as Chief Editor of the celebrated multi-volume *Oxford English Dictionary*, "any literate, educated person on the face of the globe is deprived if he does not know English."[25] Not surprisingly, "In virtually every country in the world foreigners are learning English to enable them to speak across frontiers in a language most likely to be understood by others."[26] By the same token it is understandable that, when they staged their massive 1989 demonstrations against the regime, the Chinese students – many of whom already knew English anyhow – found it valuable to carry numerous banners and placards inscribed in

132

that language. The students appreciated the fact that they were being televised worldwide, and they realized that English provided the ideal vehicle for influencing world opinion.

For a developing country like China or Indonesia or countless others, English is vital for internal purposes as well as for interactions with the rest of the world. "As well as being the language of international trade and finance, it is the language of technology, especially computers, of medicine, of the international aid bodies like Oxfam and Save the Children, and of virtually all international, quasi-diplomatic exchanges from UNESCO, to the WHO, to the UN, to Miss World, to the Olympic Committee, to world summits."[27]

English, then, is a world language of unique richness and vitality. But it is also a language of enormous power in a very special sense. Although it would be totally absurd to contend that English is the only language capable of expressing democratic concepts, it is nonetheless superlatively equipped for this role. English can indeed be called the language of democracy, and it was Winston Churchill who especially championed this identification. "We must," he said, "never cease to proclaim in fearless tones the great principles of freedom and the rights of man, which are the joint inheritance of the English-speaking world and which, through Magna Carta, the Bill of Rights, the habeas corpus, trial by jury, and the English common law find their expression in the Declaration of Independence."[28] It is no accident that, in Eastern Europe for example, so many of the underground and above-ground independence documents and freedom manifestos have been promulgated to the world in English.

As McCrum and colleagues remark about that global

language, "Its genius was, and still is, essentially democratic."[29] And here we must look once more at certain confusions which still surround the subject of communicating the democratic consensus. Marshall McLuhan, to whom reference was made in Chapter 5, well symbolized those confusions. A gifted and acclaimed researcher on the mass media and kindred topics, McLuhan detected that the nature of the mass media, particularly the electronic media, could in subtle ways influence the content of what was being disseminated. Yet as Philip Marchand, McLuhan's perceptive biographer, has shown, McLuhan's views of these matters remained ambivalent.

McLuhan, early in his career, condemned advertising, industrialism and big business not to mention Marxism. He became increasingly impressed with the way in which technological change could affect all aspects of human existence, and he focused especially on communications technology. Later he was to contend that his theory of change, which emphasized the means of communication rather than those of production, would supersede Marxism.[30] Meanwhile he was arguing that modern instantaneous communications bombarded people with impressions that made the world seem irrational rather than logical or literate. As Marchand notes, "Powerful gadgets like television were all the more dangerous, in McLuhan's view, because they fascinated those who used them and often turned those users into dependents." McLuhan even went so far as to state that he wished "none of these technologies ever happened."

Yet, suggests Marchand, McLuhan "certainly would never have maintained that there was anything intrinsically evil about technology or media. . . . One simply had to be very careful about using the media, and therefore one had to understand how the media really worked. . . ."[31] McLuhan even suggested that mankind might be on the verge of a great new global culture. But increasingly, as Marchand points out, "McLuhan was struck by what he considered the absence of any overall theory of communication. . . ."[32]

The history of the social and natural sciences shows that researchers in any field need to be refreshed with developments outside their field. World events in the 1980s have signally clarified the whole matter of the relation between the communication process and the substance of what is communicated. In communicating the widening democratic consensus, the dissemination of "straight" national and international news obviously has a major role to play. But as we have seen for example in the case of the preeminently successful BBC Overseas Service, the most authentic and effective "straight" news is founded squarely on *a bedrock of values*. These values most notably include free speech and parliamentary democracy – the very sorts of values that, for instance, are increasingly being demanded throughout the Soviet Union and her empire.

The communications/consensus interaction now becomes *a self-generating process*. On the one hand, the substratum of freedom is essential to the very process of reliable newsgathering and global news dissemination. And on the other hand the process of communicating reliable news (plus features and other programming) around the world serves to illuminate and enhance the widening democratic consensus. Here we find progress that is both mutually-reinforcing and cumulative. One can see it happening week by week, month by month, year by year.

The global communications matrix is in the best sense an *interactive* one. What happens say in Poland or Estonia can, through the communications matrix, directly influence the situation say in China, and vice versa. Constructive developments in the field of glasnost and perestroika can be communicated to every part of the world. Human rights abuses can be identified, monitored, and publicized. For these purposes, the power — we dare say the democratic power — of the inter-cultural English language can be deployed along with other appropriate languages. Thus we can communicate the broadening consensus so that no part of the world will long remain immune.

9 Power to the People

In the course of a visit to the Soviet Union in mid-1989, I again recalled what my father had so often said to me when I was a small child. In 1921 the late Herbert Hoover had sent my father to the recently-born Soviet Union, when it was gripped by famine – largely induced by Lenin's policies – and by civil war, and when Lenin had already instituted his Red Terror. My father always spoke of his admiration for the Russian people and of their stoical endurance of the privations brought about mainly by their defective system. A marvellous people with a miserable system: that was how he summed it up, and that is how one must still sum it up today.

It was on that same visit, in the opera house in the historic Ukrainian city of Kiev, that I saw and heard a brilliant performance of Puccini's "La Bohème" – perhaps the finest operatic performance I have ever experienced. This brought home to me once again the deep cultural foundations of the Russian people and their long-standing cultural links with the West. Whatever the Soviet system may be, those cultural links are indeed indissoluble.

At the same time, however, the specific Soviet political and economic system is far from indissoluble. Scientists dispute about the extent of global climatic change linked to the Greenhouse Effect; but as to the extent of change in the global political climate there can be little doubt. A counter-totalitarian tide is sweeping the world.

The symbolism of this chapter's title provides a case in point. Only a few years ago the expression "power to the people" had a distinctly left-wing ring to it. But no longer. All the more after the brutal suppression of the democracy movement in China, totalitarian double-think has largely lost its impact and its appeal. In years past, "power to the people" was hypocritically purveyed as mental fodder by one-party states. But not now. That usage has become dated, and the "power to the people" phrase has been rehabilitated for use in the way the words were intended.

It is well at this point quickly to retrace the route which we have travelled so far. In the Introduction we noted that the Russians, who from the time of Peter the Great to the present day have relied upon the West for expertise, have under Mikhail Gorbachev launched an ambitious reform programme which may or may not succeed. We suggested that the West can, especially through the power of global communications, do much to help bring about a constructive outcome. In Chapter 1 we examined Gorbachev's landmark *Perestroika* book, which provides a clarion call for reform yet is based squarely upon the defective Marxist ideology and upon the system installed by the now-discredited Lenin. We found that Gorbachev's reformist gamble could be viewed as presaging the eventual dismemberment of the Soviet empire with its flawed system. In Chapter 2 we reviewed the events attending the creation of the post-World War II Stalinist version of that empire. We found that Gorbachev's efforts to keep the empire intact are fraught with increasing difficulties, and that meanwhile the West is groping towards strategies designed to help reinforce the Soviet Union's reformist tendencies.

In Chapter 3 we briefly chronicled the evolution of communications in the context of the Soviet Union's having become the world's leading space power and the one possessing the largest satellite launch capability. We found that the dramatic growth of global satellite and other communications systems carries profound implications for ideological and cultural interactions. In Chapter 4 we viewed the growth of international broadcasting with special reference to the enormously successful BBC Overseas Service with its largest-of-all international audience. We found that the BBC's achievement derives largely from its programmes being based implicitly but squarely on the values of parliamentary democracy and human rights. In Chapter 5 we considered how, especially with the aid of satellites and sohisticated remote-sensing techniques, important physical and cultural features on the planet Earth can be delineated and how these shade into geopolitical characteristics. We found that the world is being re-mapped in more ways than one, including a growing range of economic and political common denominators.

In Chapter 6 we scrutinized the way in which space is now dominated by the needs of the military, with around three-quarters of all satellites being reserved for military purposes and with the superpowers giving much thought to how to protect their satellites and how to neutralize "enemy" satellites and missiles. We found, paradoxically enough, that the best protection may ultimately be afforded by the persuasive and peace-generating power of the messages carried by the global communications network. In Chapter 7 we observed some of the effects of uncritical Westernization including the Western Marxist ideology imposed throughout the Soviet empire as well as in diverse other parts of the world. We found that that ideology is very rapidly losing its appeal in favour of a widening global consensus based on human rights, democratic principles, and mixed-economy concepts. In Chapter 8 we took up the matter of communicating the consensus so that it can spread still more effectively. We found that, in spite of the wide recourse to disinformation and deception, the global communications process – including the mobilization of the English language in support of it – can dramatically assist in extending the consensus.

According to former President Ronald Reagan, in his Churchill Lecture in London in 1989, "more than armies, more than diplomacy, more than the best intentions of democratic nations, the communications revolution will be the greatest force for the advancement of human freedom the world has ever seen." Referring to democracy as "an intoxicant," he added:

> The biggest of big brothers is increasingly helpless against communications technology. Information is the oxygen of the modern age. The peoples of the world have increasing access to this knowledge. It seeps through the walls topped with barbed wire. It wafts across the electrified, booby-trapped borders.[1]

But what about the power of reactionary regimes which can, at least temporarily, use brute force to suppress freedom? For example, when Reagan spoke, the Peking (or Beijing) Massacre in Tiananmen Square had already happened, and in his view "those heroic

Chinese students who gave their lives have released the spirit of democracy and it cannot be called back."[2] Roderick MacFarquhar of Harvard, commenting on the role of China's so-called People's Liberation Army, has suggested that "The indiscriminate slaughter of hundreds, perhaps thousands of fellow citizens by troops of the PLA in the heart of the capital was a tragic act of monumental folly." Carrying his analysis further, he has pointed out that "The imperial political structure of China, so ably reclothed in Leninist-Maoist garb by the CCP, is crumbling, the bureaucracy is deligitimized, and the Communist ideology is discredited. . . ." And then, commenting on the overall role of China's Communist Party, MacFarquhar comes to the crux of the communications matter as follows:

> . . . During the past forty years, the CCP has visited far greater disasters upon its long-suffering people: the campaign of the early 1950s resulted in at least 800,000 executions; the Great Leap Forward caused up to 28 million deaths; the Cultural Revolution, perhaps another half million. By these standards, the Tiananmen massacre may seem a minor mishap. But it was the first time that the regime turned its guns on peacefully demonstrating people in Beijing *with the world and the rest of China looking on.* . . .[3]

The Chinese regime showed that it could excel in disinformation and deception. The regime officially insisted – in the face of eyewitness on-the-spot accounts by Western correspondents – that what the West had come to know as the Peking Massacre had never actually happened. Not a single student, said the regime's spokesmen, had been killed. And soon the

141

regime launched a programme of brutal repression which included both executions and the cynical deployment of the power of television. As one responsible journal expressed it,

> Terror by television has become the latest refinement of the inventive Chinese mind. Repressive regimes normally go to great lengths to hide the beatings and torture administered by their police and secret services. In China, the victims are being paraded on the small screen.

> Young students and workers, branded as 'thugs, counter-revolutionaries and bandits,' their faces bruised, guns held to their heads, sign confessions of non-existent crimes for the benefit of the cameras. Announcers invite the people, who know that to be arrested in China is to be convicted, to telephone a hotline to turn other 'gangsters' in for similar treatment.

> The aim is twofold – to lie about the past and to show who controls the future, at least the immediate future. . . . The 'big lie' drums home the big truth – that the party, the 'thought police' and the military are back in command.[4]

At about the same time, Deng Xiaoping, China's then paramount leader, made a speech urging much more strenuous efforts to enforce ideological unity. According to Deng much more emphasis would be placed on four basic principles: the dictatorship of the proletariat, the supremacy of the Communist Party, socialism, and the supremacy of Marxism-Leninism and Mao Tse-tung's thoughts. In Deng's view the only possible shortcoming of the party in recent years had been a neglect of ideological education along the foregoing lines.[5]

142

Deng was in effect calling for a re-emphasis of the very sorts of principles which had become thoroughly discredited throughout most of the rest of the world. And the regime was mobilizing its communications resources to help in imposing those discredited principles.

Fortunately the communications revolution works both ways. Foreign radio broadcasts can be picked up in much of China, and the BBC Overseas Service had recently – with the aid of satellite relays to the Far East – completed a massive upgrading of the strength and sweep of its signals into China. Direct international telephone dialling was operating into and out of certain of China's cities; and in diverse other Chinese cities courageous telephone operators were letting international calls through in both directions. The regime faced the danger that its fundamental guiding principles would seem increasingly ridiculous throughout China and virtually everywhere else in the world as well. But since China lacked any effective version of glasnost, this process would take time.

In the Soviet Union, on the other hand, one saw evidence of a very different situation. The world communications network of course includes books and journals as well as the electronic media, and two examples powerfully illustrated the changing Soviet political and cultural environment. Mid-1989 saw the publication, within the Soviet Union, of the first journal instalments of Alexander Solzhenitsyn's long-banned book *The Gulag Archipelago*,[6] his searing exposé of the Soviet system of labour camps especially under Stalin. And perhaps even more remarkable was the publication, within the Soviet Union and at about the same time, of the initial instalments of Vasily Grossman's long-banned novel *Forever Flowing*,[7] his moving semi-autobiographical account

143

of a Soviet citizen living in the Stalinist and post-Stalinist Soviet Union and struggling to retain his dignity as a human being.

That citizen, Ivan Grigoryevich, reflects, for example, on one of Stalin's show trials in which a group of doctors, although probably completely innocent, were forced to confess their guilt and presumably were executed – all in the name of the people. In that case, as in so many others, the real criminal was Stalin. Then in due course Stalin died. "The countryside which had groaned beneath the iron weight of Stalin's hand sighed with relief."[8] As for Lenin, "All the triumphs of Party and state were bound up with the name of Lenin. But all the cruelty inflicted on the nation also lay – tragically – on Lenin's shoulders." Moreover,

> Lenin's intolerance, Lenin's implacable drive to achieve his purpose, his contempt for freedom, his cruelty toward those who held different opinions, and his capacity to wipe off the face of the earth, without trembling, not only fortresses, but entire counties, districts, and provinces that questioned his orthodox truth – all these were characteristic of . . . Lenin. And they had deep roots.

> All his talents, all his will and his passion, were directed to one purpose – to seize power.

> To this end he sacrificed everything. And to this end – to seize power – he offered as a sacrifice, he killed, what was most sacred in Russia: Russia's freedom. . . .[10]

Such passages as these are dynamite. And mark my words: the battle to unmask and deligitimize Lenin might itself be enough to help precipitate a coup in the

Soviet Union. But the Russian people have deep and rich and abiding cultural roots, and we can hope that wiser heads will prevail. Clearly the deligitimizing process is an historically necessary one, and it must be carried out as painlessly as possible. Moreover, we who are friends of the Russian people can help this to happen. The problem of extirpating the damaging Lenin mythology is rather akin to that of dealing with an abscessed tooth: decisive steps may be needed to remove it, but the removal should be carried out with optimum surgical skill and with all appropriate medication.

What if the Soviet Union should suffer a reaction such as that in China? This is entirely conceivable and it would pose a very serious problem indeed – for the Soviet people and for the world at large. One can hope that Soviet glasnost has passed, or will soon pass, that *critical point* beyond which such a misfortune will become progressively less likely. There is no guarantee that this is or will be the case, but there are reasonable grounds for optimism. Meanwhile there are various steps which the West can take which can reinforce the prospects for a constructive outcome.

Speaking in Brussels on the occasion of the 1989 NATO summit meeting there, George Bush declared as folllows: "Our overall aim is to overcome the division of Europe and to forge a unity *based on Western values.*"[11] Bush's reiterated emphasis on enduring Western values provides a refreshing contrast to the superficial pragmatism which we referred to in Chapter 7. It likewise contrasts sharply and pleasingly with the sort of dead-end so-called "value-free analysis" which was being peddled by many Western social scientists in the 1960s and even on into the 1970s. Indeed I dare suggest that Western intellectual activity has entered a new and

145

much more constructive phase and one which can help to fill the post-Marxist intellectual vacuum especially in Eastern Europe including the Soviet Union.

Subsequently, in his long and eloquent address to the Council of Europe in Strasbourg, in northeastern France, Mikhail Gorbachev set forth a position which effectively complemented that of Bush. Although Gorbachev referred with some scorn to the view that surmounting the division of Europe meant overcoming socialism, it was clear from the context of his speech that the sort of arrangements he had in mind would in practice entail friendly ideological competition. Indeed the speech boldly proposed a pan-European communications system "for equipping the European home."

In addition to calling for the creation of a trans-European express railway, Gorbachev proposed telecommunications projects which would link Western and Eastern Europe more closely together. In particular he suggested the construction of an augmented international fibre optic cable network and a pan-European satellite communication system of course including television.[12] As he saw it,

A considerable extension of cultural cooperation, a deeper interaction in the field of humanities and a new level of information exchange are needed. To put it briefly, the process of getting to know each other better should be intensified. Television could play a special role here, since it makes it possible to ensure contacts among tens and hundreds of millions of people rather than hundreds and thousands.

Gorbachev cautioned about certain dangers inherent in the widening East-West cultural cooperation. In an apparent reference to American cultural influences in Europe, he suggested that

> ... stages, screens, exhibition halls, and publishing houses are flooded with commercial pseudo-culture alien to Europe. National languages are treated with disdain. All this calls for our common attention and joint work in the spirit of respect for the true national values of each and every one.

In spite of the cultural hazards, Gorbachev went even further. He proposed joint East-West production of cinema and television films and videos "which promote national cultural achievements and the best examples of artistic creation of the past and today."[13] It did not take much imagination to contemplate that such joint productions could likewise incorporate political, economic and social subjects. Going a step further, one could visualize that some of these productions could actively explain and promote the cause of glasnost and perestroika, the success of which was so important to the future of both Gorbachev and his country. A good analogy was provided by the Anglo-Soviet space mission designed to send a British astronaut to join the Soviet Mir space station in 1991. The project was mounted by a British private enterprise consortium in collaboration with Glavcosmos, the Soviet space agency's commercial arm. A major Western advertising agency helped to publicize the project, and over 10,000 applicants for the British astronaut role came forward.[14] One can readily visualize comparable collaboration in film production relevant to the success of Gorbachev's reform programme.

It is important to grasp the magnitude and nature of

the Soviet television audience. As Ellen Mickiewicz points out,

> Within a short time, less than two decades, television has become the principal source of information – particularly about the West – for most Soviet citizens, and a mass public has been created. It has become preeminently *the* mass medium of communication. . . . The television revolution began before Mikhail Gorbachev came to power, but he has given it a new impetus and motive power. The most dramatic changes of his tenure have been made precisely in the mass media – television foremost among them – and the effects will be far-reaching. They have been set in motion to a large extent because the Soviet leadership seeks to mobilize its population for domestic economic and social reform. . . .[15]

The massive Soviet television viewing audience comprises some 150 million people, and they happen to have an obsession with the West in general and with America in particular. Regardless of whether Soviet state television consistently gives balanced and accurate portrayals of the West – and nobody can claim that it always does – the fact remains that under glasnost it has more and more felt obliged to cater to its viewers' seemingly insatiable desire for more programming focused on the West. Under Gorbachev, "the process of adapting to the new . . . information environment and shaping it as well has moved ahead very vigorously."[16] The Soviet Union's highly developed satellite broadcasting capability, as described in Chapter 3, has of course proved a great boon here, and Gorbachev has taken full advantage of it.

Mickiewicz describes "the enormous crash program

148

that brought television into virtually every home in the Soviet Union. . . . The world comes to the Soviet people mainly from the television screen. . . ." The thirst for information about the world outside the Soviet Union can be a source of apprehension among the leadership, but it cannot be ignored. Likewise Soviet television has, in response to popular demand, increasingly presented alternative points of view on major international as well as national issues – including views in opposition to official Soviet policy. Even if largely unintentionally, a Soviet media public has been created which is vitally interested in the West and has become accustomed to hearing Western viewpoints on a range of issues.[17] This in turn opens the way to a wider constructive Western influence in aid of perestroika.

Not the least important result of the impact of television – "the most massive of mass media" – on the Soviet citizenry is that it has rendered the role of the Communist political agitator more and more obsolete. The public have become so well informed that the local party activist and his dogmas are regarded as increasingly redundant. In what many reactionaries would think of as the good old days, the activists would brainwash the people to secure constant adherence to the approved party line.[18] Those who did not conform could be consigned to a labour camp. But now, to an astonishing degree, the people have learned to think for themselves. The struggle for the hearts and minds of the people has taken a radically new turn.

It has become fashionable in the West to view Mikhail Gorbachev as a brave man struggling valiantly against the Communist old guard – and particularly against the powerful entrenched state bureaucracy – in a bid to rescue his country from political stagnation and economic collapse. In this struggle, according to the fashionable view, he could rely on the moral support not only of many well-wishers abroad but also of the Soviet citizenry at large. It would be comforting if the fashionable view were correct, but unfortunately it is not. For millions of ordinary Soviet citizens have had reason to doubt the feasibility, and even the desirability, of many of Gorbachev's reforms.

According to the Soviet sociologist Tatyana I. Zaslavskaya,

> The working class constitutes the largest group in [Soviet] socialist society. Restructuring of social relations is in its interest. . . .

> But perestroika also brings certain disadvantages to the workers, which cannot be ignored: inevitable price increases for staple foodstuffs and services up to the level which will make their production and supply . . . profitable; stepped-up rent rates . . . ; and so on. A potential cutting down of redundant jobs raises a spectrum of problems no less involved. This is a natural result of perestroika, the 'social price' which has to be paid for the acceleration of social and economic development in this country, for getting rid of our backwardness.[19]

The bulk of the working class, she adds, "do not yet have a deep understanding of the concepts of perestroika; they have not yet grasped how its measures interrelate, or how much it supports their own basic interests." Clearly, therefore, "*the mechanism for retarding perestroika* is not created by bureaucrats alone." A careful survey indicated that in 1988 only one in four or five

150

rank and file workers supported perestroika without reservations and expected positive results within two or three years. Others doubted its success or expected results only in the distant future. Only a quarter of those polled thought it necessary to restructure their own ways. Not surprisingly she concludes that perestroika "will cost intense struggle and profound conflicts of group interests."[20]

With reference to Mikhail Gorbachev, George Bush has stated categorically as follows: "I want to see him succeed."[21] By extension, Bush was in effect saying that, if Gorbachev should falter in his efforts, or if he should be unceremoniously displaced as has happened to more than one of his predecessors, then Bush would like to see an able and reform-minded successor or successors carry the torch in his place. The architecture of perestroika is, as we have seen earlier in this book, far from perfect. But if the Soviet Union is to emerge from its paradoxical status as an economically underdeveloped superpower with an underdeveloped political culture, then the Gorbachev perestroika/glasnost programme must be supported as an interim solution. It can be revised and improved as it goes along.

If, for good and sufficient reasons, a "Marshall Plan" for the Soviet Union is ruled out, there still remain major promising options through which the West can help the Gorbachev-inspired programme to suceed. Essentially the problem divides itself into two parts. The first involves taking advantage of glasnost to sell the perestroika concept to the Soviet people at large. In political terms, Gorbachev *has no adequate constituency*. The people must be galvanized and mobilized to provide political support for what he is trying to do and what like-minded successors will seek to do after him. It is here that the national and global communications network can really come into its own. It can be used to build up a groundswell of support for Gorbachev and his policies.

But it is one thing to win acceptance for the Gorbachev-inspired policies and it is quite another thing to assure their successful implementation. This is the second task, and in this realm the West can provide a virtually unlimited supply of supporting expertise. And it is here that the national and global communications network can once again come into its own. Just as it can be used to mobilize political support, so it can also be marshalled to help deliver the expertise required to make the prestroika promises come true.

The opportunities here are so legion that this book can deal with them only in indicative fashion. First it is well to return for a moment to Gorbachev's already-mentioned warning about Western cultural influences. Anybody with a sense of cultural integrity can sympathize with his general point particularly as regards America. But the massive and overt nature of America's television programme output should not blind one to the values and virtues and knowhow that can be distilled out of it. For example, in the assessment of Raymond B. Gallagher, "American television, contrary to popular opinion, features more overall programme choice than anywhere else in the world. Furthermore, this includes both entertainment and non-entertainment programming. . . ."[22] Through international satellite broadcasts into the Soviet Union, and through Soviet importation of relevant video cassettes, a significant segment of America's television output can be brought to bear to help mobilize support for perestroika and to facilitate its effective implementation.

Valuable portions of the television output of other Western countries can be made available in the same way.

In mid-1989, Western Europe's largest communications satellite, known as Olympus, was successfully launched by the European Space Agency and placed into orbit. A satellite of great power, it was equipped with two solar panels *each the size of a tennis court.* A major purpose in launching this big bird was to provide education and business footprints extending into Eastern as well as Western Europe. More than 300 educational and other institutions, from 20 countries, were involved with this project.[23]

In Chapter 3 we noted that as early as 1985 the Soviet Union signed a cooperation agreement with Turner Broadcasting of Atlanta. In 1989 Turner Broadcasting negotiated an agreement with the Russian authorities to extend regular CNN global news broadcasts to subscription customers in the Soviet Union.[24] This provided a further example of the wide scope for East-West collaboration in broadcasting; and such a collaboration could feature objective and persuasive programmes of direct relevance to the success of perestroika.

Among the fields in which substantive collaboration is especially needed are public relations and advertizing, public administration, and business administration, together with the one-world English language. Expertise in public relations and advertizing can help widen popular support for perestroika; and the Soviet Union desperately needs expertise to help bring improved management to both the public and quasi-private sectors. "Shortages," as Padma Desai has pointed out, "breed alienation."[25] It is vital to get to the bottom of such shortages – whether of meat or matches or soap or whatever – and to eliminate the administrative roadblocks which cause them. To make perestroika work, the Soviet ministries, as well as the joint ventures and cooperatives, can benefit enormously both from broadcasts devoted to sound management and from visits by teams of Western "bottleneck-busters" experienced in weeding out administrative inefficiencies. In 1989 the United Kingdom, through its British Council and with the help of the British private sector, launched a programme to help the Soviet Union with administrative improvement,[26] and various other Western countries are doing likewise. The whole process needs to be accelerated if it is not to be too late.

In Chapter 6 we noted Joseph Frankel's valuable and suggestive analysis which regards state power as "a potential for influence." For over seventy years the Soviet Union, with her rich and priceless cultures, has been going through a series of cycles which have hitherto never brought durable freedom to her own people or to those within her empire. But now the potential for constructive influence has been vastly enhanced through the power of the global system of communications, in which the Soviet Union has herself latterly become a major player. Ronald Reagan may in historical perspective be forgiven for his statement that "the communications revolution will be the greatest force for the advancement of human freedom the world has ever seen." And regardless of the outcome, few situations could offer more excitement than that which is unfolding in the Soviet Union and throughout Eastern and Central Europe.

Notes

PREFACE
  1 Donald Wilhelm, *Creative Alternatives to Communism: Guidelines for Tomorrow's World* (London: The Macmillan Press Ltd., 1977). The work was published in both hardback and paperback in 1977 and reprinted in hardback and paperback in 1977 and again in 1978.

INTRODUCTION
  1 Mikhail Gorbachev, *Perestroika: New Thinking for Our Country and the World* (London: William Collins & Co. Ltd., 1987).

CHAPTER 1   THE PERILS OF PERESTROIKA
  1 Gorbachev, op. cit., pp. 18–29, 23–4.
  2 Ibid., p. 66.
  3 Ibid., p. 11.
  4 Ibid., p. 155.
  5 Andrei D. Sakharov, *Sakharov Speaks* (London: Collins & Harvill Press, 1974), pp. 124–210.
  6 Ronald W. Clark, *Lenin: The Man Behind the Mask* (London: Faber and Faber, 1988).
  7 Ibid., pp. 301–8.
  8 Ibid., pp. 376–7.
  9 Idem.
10 Robert Conquest, *Lenin* (London: Fontana/Collins, 1972), pp. 98, 100.
11 Francoise Thom and David Regan, *Glasnost, Gorbachev and Lenin* (London: Policy Research Pubications Ltd., 1988), p.52.
12 Clark, op. cit., p. 415.
13 Conquest, op. cit., p. 107.
14 *The Daily Telegraph* (London), 31 October 1988, p. 13.

15 *The Times* (London), 31 October 1988, p. 10.
16 Clark, op. cit., p. 472.
17 Ibid., p. 474.
18 Ibid., p. 492.
19 Conquest, op. cit., p. 129.
20 Gorbachev, op. cit., p. 36.
21 Ibid., p. 37.
22 Ibid., p. 86.
23 Sakharov, op. cit., pp. 12–13.
24 Ibid., p. 86.
25 Jacques Rupnik, *The Other Europe* (London: Weidenfeld and Nicholson, 1988), p. 21.
26 Karl Marx, *Capital: A Critical Analysis of Capitalist Production* (Moscow: Progress Publishers, 1974), Vol. I, p. 173.
27 *Marxism, Communism and Western Society: A Comparative Encyclopedia* (New York: Herder and Herder, 1973), Vol. VII, pp. 36–7.
28 Marx, *Capital*, op. cit., Vol. II, pp. 36–7.
29 Karl Marx, *The Poverty of Philosophy* (Moscow: Progress Publishers, 1973), p. 95.
30 Karl Marx and Friedrich Engels, *The Communist Manifesto* (Harmondsworth, Middlesex: Penguin Books, 1975), pp. 79, 121.
31 Ibid., p. 85.
32 Ibid., pp. 86–7.
33 See, e.g., C. R. Fay, *Palace of Industry, 1851: A Study of the Great Exhibition and Its Fruits* (Cambridge, England: Cambridge University Press, 1951).
34 *The Times* (London), 8 November 1988, p. 24.
35 Thom and Regan, op. cit., p. 34.
36 Clark, op. cit., p. 430.
37 Quoted in ibid., p. 437.
38 Ibid., pp. 433–7.
39 Geoffrey Hosking, "A Great Power in Crisis," in *The Listener* (London), 10 November 1988, p. 19.
40 BBC News, 4 November 1988.

CHAPTER 2   REINFORCING REFORM
1 Jacques Rupnik, *The Other Europe* (London: Weidenfeld and Nicolson, 1988), p. 266.
2 Karen Dawisha, *Eastern Europe, Gorbachev and Reform* (Cambridge, England: Cambridge University Press, 1988), p. 169.
3 Rupnik, op. cit., pp. 59, 227.
4 Geoffrey Hosking, "The Flawed Melting-Pot," in *The Listener* (London), 1 December 1988, p. 16.

5 Rupnik, op. cit., p. 68.

6 Hosking, idem.

7 Tim Whewell, "The Gorbachev Decade," in The Economist, *The World in 1989* (London: The Economist, 1988), p. 52.

8 *Financial Times* (London), 2 December 1988, p. 2.

9 Whewell, idem.

10 Whewell, "Those Bolshy Balts," in op. cit., p. 49.

11 Whewell, "The Gorbachev Decade," in op. cit., p. 48.

12 Michael Dockrill, *The Cold War, 1945–1963* (London: Macmillan Education Ltd., 1988), p. 17.

13 Julius W. Pratt, *A History of United States Foreign Policy* (2nd ed., Englewood Cliffs, N.J.: Prentice-Hall, Inc., 1965), p. 426.

14 John Terraine, *The Mighty Continent* (London: British Broadcasting Corporation, 1974), p. 260.

15 Zygmunt C. Szkopiak, Ed., *The Yalta Agreements* (London: The Polish Government in Exile, 1988), pp. 20–1.

16 Pratt, op. cit., p. 430.

17 Rupnik, op. cit., p. 67.

18 Ibid., p. 72.

19 Pratt, op. cit., p. 455.

20 George F. Kennan, *Russia and the West Under Lenin and Stalin* (London: Hutchinson & Co. Ltd., 1961), pp. 361–2.

21 J. Robert Wegs, *Europe Since 1945: A Concise History* (2nd ed., London: Macmillan Education Ltd., 1984), p. 8.

22 Rupnik, op. cit., p. 71.

23 *The Economist* (London), 17 December 1988, p. 12.

24 Thomas Sherlock, "Politics and History under Gorbachev," in *Problems of Communism* (Washington, D.C.), May–August 1988, p. 17.

25 Ibid., pp. 40–1.

26 John W. Spanier, "Cold War," in *The Encyclopedia Americana* (Danbury, Conn.: Americana Corporation, 1979), vol. 7, p. 222.

27 Walter Laqueur, *Europe Since Hitler* (rev. ed., New York: Viking Penguin Inc., 1987), p. 381.

28 Wegs, op. cit., pp. 136–7.

29 Marshall D. Shulman, *Stalin's Foreign Policy Reappraised* (Cambridge, Mass.: Harvard University Press, 1963).

30 Quoted by R. N. Carew Hunt in *A Guide to Communist Jargon* (London: Bles, 1957), p. 32.

31 Mikhail Gorbachev, *Perestroika* (London: William Collins Sons & Co. Ltd., 1987), p. 148.

32 Ibid., p. 47.

33 Daniel Bell, *The End of Ideology* (New York: The Free Press, 1962).

34 Vo Nguyen Giap, *People's War, People's Army* (Hanoi: Foreign Languages Publishing House, 1974).
35 Pratt, op. cit., pp. 471–5.

CHAPTER 3   THE SATELLITE EXPLOSION
 1 Royal Institute of International Affairs, *Europe's Future in Space* (London: Routledge & Kegan Paul, 1988), p. 23.
 2 Harry Edward Neal, *Communication: From Stone Age to Space Age* (London: Phoenix House Ltd., 1960), p. 51.
 3 Peter M. Lewis and Corinne Pearlman, *Media & Power* (London: Camden Press, 1986), p. 12.
 4 Neal, op. cit., p. 83.
 5 Quoted in ibid., p. 98.
 6 Ibid., p. 106.
 7 Ibid., pp. 109–21.
 8 Ibid., pp. 121–4.
 9 Ibid., pp. 126–7.
10 Ibid., pp. 128–30.
11 Ibid., pp. 131–2.
12 Gordon Ross, *Television Jubilee* (London: W. H. Allen, 1961), p. 128.
13 Joseph N. Pelton, in Mark Long, *World Satellite Almanac* (2nd ed., Indianapolis: Howard W. Sams & Company, 1987), p. xvi.
14 Royal Institute of International Affairs, op. cit., pp. 4, 25.
15 Long, op. cit., p. 3.
16 Quoted by Ross, op. cit., pp. 21–2.
17 Long, op. cit., p. 9.
18 Ibid., p. 57.
19 Ibid., pp. 57–9.
20 Ibid., p. 81.
21 Ibid., p. 88.
22 Ibid., p. 99.
23 Ibid., pp. 105ff.
24 Ibid., pp. 117f.
25 Ibid., pp. 123–5.
26 Donald Wilhelm, *Emerging Indonesia* (2nd ed., London: Quiller Press Limited, 1985), p. 157; Long, op. cit., pp. 125–7.
27 Long, op. cit., pp. 131ff.
28 Royal Institute of International Affairs, op. cit., p. 25.
29 Ibid., p. 15.
30 *Financial Times* (London), 25 January 1989, p. 3.

CHAPTER 4   CULTURAL CHAOS?

1 *Evening Standard* (London), 25 January 1989, p. 12.
2 Quoted in Tom Burns, *The BBC: Public Institution and Private World* (London: The Macmillan Press, Ltd., 1979), p. 36.
3 Idem. Cf. also Roger Milner, *Reith: The BBC Years* (Edinburgh: Mainstream Publishing Company Ltd., 1983).
4 Quoted in Gerard Mansell, *Let the Truth Be Told: 50 Years of BBC External Broadcasting* (London: Weidenfeld and Nicolson,1982), pp. 2, 22.
5 Mansell, op. cit., p. 195.
6 Ibid., p. 61.
7 Ibid., p. 104.
8 Quoted in ibid., p. 211.
9 John Tusa et al., *Voice for the World* (London: BBC World Service, 1988), p. 18.
10 Ibid., p. 15.
11 J. M. Mitchell, *International Cultural Relations* (London: Allen & Unwin, 1986), p. 5.
12 House of Commons, Foreign Affairs Committee, Session 1986–87, *Minutes of Evidence*, 14 January 1987 (London: Her Majesty's Stationery Office, 1987), p. 111.
13 Quoted in John Tusa in "The Problems of Freedom and Responsibility in Broadcasting," address at the University College of North Wales, 25 June 1988, pp. 4–5.
14 *Universal Declaration of Human Rights: Final Authorized Text* (New York: United Nations Office of Information, 1972), pp. 3–6.
15 Quoted in Ivor Jennings, *The Queen's Government* (Harmondsworth, Middlesex: Penguin Books, 1954), p. 9. See also G. R. C. Davis, *Magna Carta* (London: The Trustees of the British Museum, 1971).
16 Tusa et al., *Voice for the World*, op. cit., pp. 4–5; *Financial Times* (London), 12 January 1988, p. 2.
17 Tusa et al., *Voice for the World*, op. cit., p. 5.
18 J. Crispin et al., "Satellites Versus Fibre Optic Cables," *International Journal of Satellite Communications* (Chichester, England, 1985) Vol. 3, 217–20.
19 *Financial Times*, idem.
20 Based on Voice of America, *VOA Today* (Washington, D.C., Voice of America, n.d.) and other VOA releases.
21 The Board for International Broadcasting, *1989 Annual Report on Radio Free Europe/Radio Liberty, Inc.* (Washington, D.C.: The Board for International Broadcasting, 1989), p. 10.
22 Radio Free Europe/Radio Liberty, Inc., *The RFE/RL Professional*

Code (Washington, D.C.: Radio Free Europe/Radio Liberty, Inc., n.d.), p. 2.

23 *Le Pointe* (Paris), 5 September 1988, "Radio Free Europe: Shock Waves," translated article, p. 2.
24 *Sueddeutsche Zeitung* (Munich), 5 September 1988, "Glasnost in the Ether," translated article, p. 1.
25 *VOA Today*, op. cit., p. 9.
26 Based on various releases of Reuters Holdings PLC, London.
27 Based on Visnews Ltd. releases.
28 Based on Worldwide Television News releases.

CHAPTER 5   RE-MAPPING THE WORLD

1 *International Encyclopedia of the Social Sciences* (London: Collier-Macmillan Publishers, 1968), Vol. 6, pp. 131, 138.
2 Eugene C. Hargrove, Ed., *Beyond Spaceship Earth* (San Francisco: Sierra Club Books, 1986), pp. ix–xv.
3 In ibid., pp. 20–1 (italics added).
4 In ibid., pp. 22–3.
5 In ibid., p. 32.
6 Paul J. Curran, *Principles of Remote Sensing* (New York: John Wiley & Sons, Inc., 1985), p. 139.
7 Christopher Mueller-Wille et al., *Images of the World* (Glasgow: Wm. Collins Sons & Co. Ltd., 1984), p. 15.
8 Ray Harris, *Satellite Remote Sensing* (London: Routledge & Kegan Paul, 1987), pp. 72–3.
9 Mueller-Wille et al., op. cit., p. 10.
10 Harris, op. cit., pp. 73–5.
11 Mueller-Wille et al., op. cit., pp. 19–160.
12 E. C. Barrett and L. F. Curtis, *Introduction to Environmental Remote Sensing* (London: Chapman and Hall, 1976), pp. 151ff.
13 Ibid., pp. 217ff.
14 Ibid., pp. 271ff.
15 Ibid., pp. 307ff.
16 C. P. Lo, *Applied Remote Sensing* (Harlow, Essex: Longman Group UK Limited, 1986), p. 40.
17 Ibid., pp. 48–50.
18 Barrett and Curtis, op. cit., pp. 298ff.
19 *International Encyclopedia of the Social Sciences*, op. cit., Vol. 6, p. 117 (italics added).
20 Idem.
21 In Hargrove, Ed., op. cit., p. 39.
22 J. P. Cole, *Geography of World Affairs* (6th ed., London: Butterworths, 1983), pp. 240–1.

23 Peter J. Taylor, *Political Geography* (Harlow, Essex: Longman Group UK Limited, 1985), pp. 29, 45.

24 Richard Muir, *Modern Political Geography* (2nd ed., London: Macmillan Education Ltd., 1987), p. 15.

25 Ibid., pp. 150, 152.

26 *International Encyclopedia of the Social Sciences*, op. cit., Vol. 6, p. 129.

27 Marshall McLuhan, *Understanding Media* (London: Routledge & Kegan Paul Ltd., 1987), pp. 7ff.

28 Carl J. Friedrich and Zbigniew K. Brzezinski, *Totalitarian Dictatorship and Autocracy* (Cambridge, Mass.: Harvard University Press, 1956), p. 303.

29 Zbigniew Brzezinski, *The Grand Failure: The Birth and Death of Communism in the Twentieth Century* (New York: Scribner's, 1989).

30 John Kenneth Galbraith and Stanislav Menshikov, *Capitalism, Communism and Coexistence* (Boston: Houghton Mifflin Company, 1988).

31 Peter Gould and Rodney White, *Mental Maps* (2nd ed., Boston: Allen & Unwin, 1986), p. 20.

32 Muir, op. cit., pp. 70–1; Peter Haggett, *Geography: A Modern Synthesis* (3rd ed., New York: Harper & Row, 1983), pp. 265, 393–7.

33 Gould and White, op. cit., pp. 82–3.

34 *International Encyclopedia of the Social Sciences*, op. cit., Vol. 12, p. 220.

35 John Lloyd in *Financial Times* (London), 4/5 March 1989, Sec. II, p. 1.

36 In Galbraith and Menshikov, op. cit., p. 140.

37 In ibid., p. 33.

38 Fred Coleman and Russell Watson in *Newsweek* (New York), 13 March 1989, p. 8.

39 In Galbraith and Menshikov, op. cit., p. 9.

40 Descartes is justly called the father of modern philosophy. See, e.g., John Cottingham, *Descartes* (Oxford: Basil Blackwell Ltd., 1986) and Tom Sorell, *Descartes* (Oxford: Oxford University Press, 1987).

CHAPTER 6   COMBINED SPACE STRATEGY

1 *The Sunday Telegraph* (London), 26 March 1989, p. 1 (exclusive interview).

2 In Ari Sternfeld et al., *Soviet Writings on Earth Satellites and Space Travel* (London: Macgibbon & Kee, 1959), p. 13.

3 In ibid., p. 199.

4 Christopher Lee, *War in Space* (London: Sphere Books Limited, 1987), p. 2.
5 In Stephen Kirby and Gordon Robson, Eds., *The Militarisation of Space* (Brighton, Sussex: Wheatsheaf Books Ltd., 1987), p. 1.
6 William E. Burrows, *Deep Space* (London: Transworld Publishers Ltd.), p. 325.
7 Rip Bulkeley and Graham Spinardi, *Space Weapons: Deterrence or Delusion?* (Cambridge, England: Polity Press, 1986), pp. 38–9.
8 Ibid., pp. 40–5.
9 Ibid., pp. 45–7.
10 Kirby and Robson, op. cit., pp. 166–7.
11 Paul B. Stares, *Space Weapons and US Strategy: Origins and Development* (Beckenham, Kent: Croom Helm Ltd., 1985), p. 238.
12 John Hackett et al., *The Third World War: August 1985* (London: Sphere Books Limited, 1987), p. 180.
13 U.S. Department of Defense, *Soviet Military Power: An Assessment of the Threat, 1988* (Washington, D.C.: Superintendent of Documents, 1988), pp. 64–5; Burows, op. cit., pp. 281–3.
14 Bulkeley and Spinardi, op. cit., pp. 49–50.
15 For the text of the relevant part of Ronald Reagan's 23 March 1983 speech announcing the SDI programme, v., e.g., Frank Barnaby, *What on Earth is Star Wars? A Guide to the Strategic Defense Initiative* (London: Fourth Estate, 1986), pp. 163–6.
16 U.S. Department of Defense, op. cit., pp. 55, 59.
17 Ibid., p. 59.
18 Barnaby, op. cit., p. 44.
19 U.S. Department of Defense, op. cit., pp. 47, 50.
20 Bulkeley and Spinardi, op. cit., p. 211.
21 Hackett et al., op. cit., pp. 234, 256.
22 In Bhupendra Jasani and Toshiba Sakata, Eds., *Satellites for Arms Control and Crisis Monitoring* (Oxford: Oxford University Press, 1987), p. 3.
23 In ibid., pp. 124ff.
24 Burrows, op. cit., pp. 324–5.
25 F. S. Northedge, *The International Political System* (London: Faber and Faber Limited, 1984), pp. 20–1.
26 Paul Kennedy, *The Rise and Fall of the Great Powers: Economic Change and Military Conflict, 1500 to 2000* (London: Unwin Hyman, 1988), p. 539.
27 Joseph Frankel, *International Relations in a Changing World* (4th ed., Oxford: Oxford University Press, 1988), pp. 11, 96.
28 Ibid., p. 111.
29 Brian Moynahan, *The Claws of the Bear: A History of the Soviet Armed*

162

Forces from 1917 to the Present (London: Century Hutchinson Ltd., 1989), p. ix.

30 Ibid., p. 333.

31 Ibid., pp. 333–4, 399.

32 Ibid., p. 428.

33 Gregory C. Radabaugh, "Soviet Antisatellite Capabilities," *Signal* (Fairfax, Virginia), December 1988, p. 81.

34 John L. Petrowski, "Soviet Space Doctrine for Warfighting," *Signal*, December 1988, p.33.

CHAPTER 7   THE CROSS-CULTURAL CONSENSUS

1 For a fascinating historical perspective see David Kunzle, *Fashion and Fetishism* (Totowa, New Jersey: Rowman and Littlefield, 1982).

2 Quoted in Donald Wilhelm, *Emerging Indonesia* (2nd ed., London: Quiller Press Limited, 1985), pp. 167–8.

3 Amir Taheri, *Holy Terror: The Inside Story of Islamic Terrorism* (London: Century Hutchinson Ltd., 1987), p. 20.

4 Wilhelm, op. cit., p. 95.

5 Ibid., pp. 95–6.

6 Ibid., pp. 158–9.

7 *The Times* (London), 6 May 1989, p. 7; *The Daily Telegraph* (London), 6 May 1989, p. 11.

8 Taheri, op. cit., p. 205.

9 Dilip Hiro, *Iran Under the Ayatollahs* (London: Routledge & Kegan Paul Ltd., 1987), pp. 291–2.

10 Saul Bakhash, *The Reign of the Ayatollahs: Iran and the Islamic Revolution* (London: Unwin Paperbacks, 1986), p. 237.

11 Zbigniew Brzezinski, *The Grand Failure: The Birth and Death of Communism in the Twentieth Century* (New York: Charles Scribner's Sons, 1989), p. 6.

12 Ibid., pp. 7, 12, 15.

13 Ibid., pp. 20, 21, 23, 25.

14 Ibid., pp. 40, 43–4.

15 Ibid., p. 45.

16 Ibid., p. 45–9.

17 Ibid., p. 50.

18 Ibid., pp. 53, 99.

19 Ibid., pp. 118–120, 130.

20 Ibid., p. 144 (italics added).

21 Ibid., pp. 155–6.

22 Ibid., p. 207.

23 Ibid., pp. 210, 231, 240, 242.

24 J. O. Urmson, in *The Concise Encyclopedia of Western Philosophy and Philosophers* (London: Hutchinson, 1975), p. 233.
25 Morton White, *Pragmatism and the American Mind* (New York: Oxford University Press, 1975), p. 95.
26 Brzezinskiy, op. cit., p. 12.
27 Seweryn Bialer and Michael Mandelbaum, *The Global Rivals: The Soviet-American Contest for Supremacy* (London: I. B. Tauris & Co. Ltd., 1989), p. 99.
28 Ibid., pp. 106, 124.
29 J. M. Roberts, *The Triumph of the West* (London: British Broadcasting Corporation, 1985), p. 412 (italics added).
30 Brzezinski, op. cit., p. 12.

CHAPTER 8   COMMUNICATING THE CONSENSUS
1 *The Daily Telegraph* (London), 25 May 1988, p. 14.
2 *Financial Times* (London), 27/28 May 1989, p. 22.
3 *International Encyclopedia of the Social Sciences* (London: Collier-Macmillan Publishers, 1968), Vol. 3, p. 90.
4 Edward Jay Epstein, *Deception: The Invisible War Between the KGB and the CIA* (New York: Simon and Schuster, 1989), p. 129 (italics added).
5 Ibid., pp. 129–31.
6 Ibid., pp. 140–3.
7 Anthony Read and David Fisher, *The Deadly Embrace: Hitler, Stalin and the Nazi-Soviet Pact, 1939–1941* (New York: W. W. Norton & Company, 1989), pp. 12–13.
8 Ronald Lewin, *Ultra Goes to War* (London: Grafton Books, 1988), p. 22.
9 *The Times* (London), 25 May 1989, p. 10.
10 *The Sunday Times* (London), 28 May 1989, pp. A1, B1.
11 Epstein, op. cit., p. 230.
12 *International Encyclopedia of the Social Sciences*, op. cit., Vol. 12, p. 579.
13 J. M. Mitchell, *International Cultural Relations* (London: Allen & Unwin, 1986), p. 28.
14 Quoted in ibid., p. 31.
15 In Richard F. Staar, Ed., *Public Diplomacy: USA Versus USSR* (Stanford, Calif.: Hoover Institution Press, 1986), p. 35.
16 In Staar, Ed., op. cit., pp. 96–7.
17 In ibid., p. 101.
18 In ibid., p. 107.
19 In ibid., p. 234.
20 Robert Burchfield, *The English Language* (Oxford: Oxford University Press, 1986), p. 2.

21 *The Holy Bible: Revised Standard Edition* (London: Oxford University Press, 1952), p. 10.

22 Simeon Potter, *Our Language* (London: Penguin Books Ltd., 1987), p. 175.

23 Robert McCrum, William Cran, and Robert MacNeil, *The Story of English* (London: Faber and Faber, 1988), pp. 19–20.

24 Ibid., pp. 38–9.

25 Quoted in ibid., p. 39.

26 Burchfield, op. cit., p. 169.

27 Crum et al., op. cit., pp. 42–3.

28 Quoted in ibid., pp. 32–3.

29 Ibid., p. 48.

30 Philip Marchand, *Marshall McLuhan: The Medium and the Messenger* (New York: Ticknor & Fields, 1989), pp. 49, 69, 145.

31 Ibid., pp. 121, 130–1.

32 Ibid., p. 231.

CHAPTER 9   POWER TO THE PEOPLE

1 Transcript of Ronald Reagan's 14 June 1989 Churchill Lecture (London: The English-Speaking Union), p. 3.

2 Idem.

3 Roderick MacFarquhar, "The End of the Chinese Revolution," *The New York Review of Books* (New York), 20 July 1989, p. 10 (italics added).

4 *The Times* (London), 13 June 1989, p. 17.

5 *Financial* Times (London), 17 June 1989, p. 2.

6 *Financial Times*, 14 July 1989, p. 1. For an abridged English-language edition, see Alexander Solzhenitsyn, *The Gulag Archipelago: 1918–1956* (London: Collins Harvill, 1988).

7 For an English-language edition, see Vasily Grossman, *Forever Flowing* (London: Collins Harvill, 1988).

8 Ibid., p. 29.

9 Ibid., p. 195.

10 Ibid., p. 203.

11 George Bush, in official transcript of post-summit news conference, Brussels, 30 May 1989, p. 1 (italics added).

12 Novosti Press Agency (London), official English-language transcript, dated 7 July 1989, of Mikhail Gorbachev's address of 6 July 1989 to the Council of Europe, Strasbourg, pp. 2, 10.

13 Ibid., pp. 13–14.

14 *The Times* (London), 11 July 1989, p. 4.

15 Ellen Mickiewicz, *Split Signals: Television and Politics in the Soviet Union* (New York: Oxford University Press, 1988), p. v.

16 Ibid., pp. vi, 5.
17 Ibid., pp. 32, 34, 35, 49.
18 Ibid., pp. 180, 200, 209–210.
19 In Abel Aganbegyan, Ed., *Perestroika Annual* (London: Futura Publications, 1988), p. 256.
20 Ibid., pp. 258, 259, 260, 277 (italics added).
21 George Bush, in op. cit., p. 3.
22 Raymond B. Gallagher, in Cento Veljanovski, Ed., *Freedom in Broadcasting* (London: The Institute of Economic Affairs, 1989), p. 190.
23 *The Daily Telegraph* (London), 13 July 1989, p. 8; European Space Agency, European Space Research and Technology Centre (Leiden, The Netherlands), press release CCB/53748/JC, June 1989.
24 *Cable and Satellite Europe* (London), June 1989, p. 14. For a biography of Ted Turner, see Christian Williams, *Lead, Follow or Get Out of the Way* (New York: Times Books, 1981).
25 Padma Desai, *Perestroika in Perspective: The Design and Dilemmas of Soviet Reform* (London: I. B. Tauris & Co. Ltd., 1989), p. 6.
26 The British Council (London), press release of 9 January 1989.

Index

168

169

Reith, John, 51–4
remote sensing, 71–5, 87–98, 139
Reuter, Paul Julius, 64
Reuters, 64
Roberts, J.M., 117–18
Robson, Gordon, 87, 89
Romania, x, 44
Roosevelt, Franklin D., 21, 22, 23
Roshco, Bernard, 129
Rupnik, Jacques, 9, 17–18, 19, 22–3, 26
Russia, xii, 3, 4, 6, 9, 24, 108, 121–2, 144
Russian Revolution, 4, 107

Sakharov, Andrei D., 2, 5, 8–9
San Marino, 47
satellites, 20, 34, 41–50, 59–60, 64–5, 68, 71–8, 85–98, 100, 139–40, 143, 146, 148, 152–3
Saudi Arabia, 47, 48
Shah of Iran, 104–6
Sherlock, Thomas, 25
Shulman, Marshall D., 27
Singapore, 48, 59
Smith, Mack, 127
Solidarity, xiii, 16, 17–18, 111
Solzhenitsyn, Alexander, 9, 27, 143
Somalia, 47
Soviet empire, xii, xiii, xiv, 7, 13, 17, 18, 19, 20, 21, 33, 63, 76, 84, 111, 112, 135, 138–9, 140, 154
Soviet Union, ix, xii, xiii, 1–9, 13, 14, 15, 16, 17, 18, 19, 21, 25, 26, 28, 29, 32, 33, 34, 42, 44, 45, 48–9, 55, 62, 63, 64, 65, 68, 69, 73, 75–6, 77, 78, 79, 81, 82–3, 84, 85–6, 88, 89, 90, 91, 92, 93, 94, 95, 96, 98,

99–101, 103, 107–14, 117, 121–2, 125–6, 129, 130–1, 135, 137–40, 143–54
spaceology, 70
Spain, 47
Spanier, John W., 26
Spinardi, Graham, 88
Sputnik, 34, 50, 76, 79, 87
Stalin, 4–5, 6, 21, 23, 25, 26, 27, 28, 29, 31, 33, 75, 109, 122–4, 143, 144
Stares, Paul B., 90
Stephenson, George, 37
Sternfield, Ari, 85–6
Stockholm International Peace Research Institute, 98
Strategic Defense Initiative, 20, 92–6
Sudan, 47
Sweden, 47, 48
Switzerland, 47, 121
Syria, 44, 47

Taheri, Amir, 103–4, 107
Taylor, Peter, J., 76–7
technology, 12–13, 64, 66, 70, 84, 86, 87, 97, 105, 116, 125, 129, 131, 134, 140
Teheran Conference, 19, 21
telegraph, 38, 64
telephone, 38–9, 143
television, 40–50, 51, 64–7, 117, 134, 142, 146, 147, 148–9, 152–3
Thailand, 48
Thatcher, Margaret, 16
Thom, Francoise, 14
transistor, 40, 42, 105
Truman Doctrine, 28
Tunisia, 47
Turkey, 47
Turner Broadcasting, 45, 153
Tusa, John, 56–7